"The longstanding assumption
tians are to be quiet and weak b
churches, our relationships, and,
In this in-depth and faithful exposition of the third beatitude,
Davy Ellison challenges that false assumption. Instead, based
on Jesus' life, ministry, teaching, and example, Ellison calls us
to live in true meekness. Grounded in who we are in Jesus, empowered by his Spirit, and with his mindset of humility, we are
to act with inner strength for the good of others and the glory
of God. If you want to be encouraged by faithful exposition that
makes helpful application, you will want to read *Meekness and
Majesty*."

Juan Sanchez
Senior Pastor, High Pointe Baptist Church;
Author of *The Leadership Formula*

"In a world where people either tend to be squishy and weak
or shrill and mean, and where many erroneously believe 'the
powerful will inherit the earth,' Davy Ellison delivers a needed
book on meekness. Through engaging illustrations, explanations, and arguments, he helps combat the misconception that
meekness is weakness. This book will encourage you to walk on
the Calvary Road in the footsteps of the meek and lowly Nazarene knowing we too who walk in meekness will one day 'inherit the earth.'"

Nate Akin
Executive Director, The Pillar Network;
Director, Baptist 21

"Meekness is perhaps the least talked about, but most needed virtue in our Christian culture today. In an age of celebrity pastors and leaders, Davy Ellison gives a fresh and encouraging look at the type of people Christ calls us to be. This book will challenge and convict, and point you to the upside down kingdom Christ brings."

Courtney Reissig
Author, *Teach Me To Feel:*
Worshipping Through the Psalms in Every Season of Life

"Let me start where Davy Ellison ends, 'The paradoxical promise remains: "Blessed are the meek, for they shall inherit the earth" (Matt.5:5).' The paradoxical promise—what a great expression to summarise the theme of this very readable and accessible, but thought provoking and somewhat hard-hitting book. And how relevant the subject. Meekness is very much out of vogue, whether it be in the offices of corporate business, the hallways of political power or the arenas of professional sport. And sadly, it is out of vogue even within the triumphalistic, ego-centred, self-absorbed lives of many in the Christian church. How few within the church, dare I say, especially amongst leaders in the church, how few are truly meek. And, possibly more soberly, how few even desire to be meek. I hope that through this book many would be willing to play the waiting game of meekness, in the expectation that the paradoxical promise is indeed true."

John Bell
Pastor, Covenanters Christian Church,
Harare, Zimbabwe

"In this volume, Davy Ellison provides a biblical-theological exploration of the theme of meekness, locating Jesus' call for meekness within the Bible's redemptive storyline from creation to new creation and showing how Jesus himself is the meek one *par excellence*. How would our lives, our churches, our witness be different if we all grew in godly meekness? Read this book to see the Bible's call to a counter-intuitive, upside-down way of living. Read it if you long to inherit the earth."

Stephen Witmer
Author, *Eternity Changes Everything*;
Council member of The Gospel Coalition

Meekness and Majesty

For
Desi Alexander, Sarah Dalrymple and Tom Moore.

All three of you have been significant influences on me in recent years and in each of you I have witnessed the meekness and gentleness of Christ. The Lord has used this to shape me and for that gift I am immensely grateful.

S.D. Ellison

Meekness & Majesty

H&E
Publishing

H&E Publishing
West Lorne, Ontario, Canada
www.hesedandemet.com

Paperback ISBN: 978-1-77484-144-0
eBook ISBN: 978-1-77484-145-7

CONTENTS

Foreword

Stop! Before you continue reading, I want to ask you a question: What does it mean to be "meek"? Try to define it in your own words.

I bet you struggled a bit. I bet you found it easier to define what it is *not* rather than what it is. If you define it like most people—as mousy, weak, inconsequential—I think you're off target, at least according to the Bible and what Jesus had to say about those who are meek.

Why do we often get the definition of this important idea wrong, especially as Christians? Why do we pray so little about meekness? Why are so few sermons preached on it? After all, the inheritance of the earth is at stake, right?

I can guess why. As someone born in the U.S., I can tell you that meekness is not a very American idea. If it ever was, it has been lost for decades. Netflix documentaries feature the courageous. Social media "likes" the ridiculous. Attention goes to the brazen. The aggressor takes the cake. Not the meek. Never the meek. Or so it seems.

Matthew Henry, a 17th-century pastor, has the best definition of meekness that I've ever heard. Not only the best, but also the most challenging:

> These meek ones are here represented as happy, even in this world. They are blessed, for they are like the blessed Jesus. They are like blessed God himself, who is Lord of his anger, and in whom fury is not. They are blessed, for they have the most comfortable, undisturbed enjoyment of themselves, their friends, their God; they are fit for

any relation, and condition, any company; fit to live, and fit to die.

That sounds nothing like weak and mousy! No, it sounds like a challenge, a calling. Oh, that Christ's church would be meek! That all God's people would understand meekness and walk in it!

Davy Ellison has helped us take a giant step forward in our understanding of what it means to be meek. Gain from his wisdom and make it your own. May God make you fit to live and fit to die.

Matt Schmucker
Washington, DC
2023

Introduction:
Taking Issue with Jesus

"Blessed are the meek, for they shall inherit the earth" (Matt. 5:5). I take issue with these words, and I know who spoke them. But before you begin shaking your head and tutting at me disapprovingly, you too take issue with Jesus. Everyone takes issue with the message of Jesus at this point. We do so because there is one primary problem with Jesus' declaration: no-one wants to be known as meek.

If I am honest, I do not want to be known as meek. If you are honest with yourself, you do not want to be known as meek. No one does. Meekness is a trait seldom if ever valued in modern society. It is a characteristic we rarely look for in one another. Consider the last application form you completed, or job interview you attended; I doubt you were asked to demonstrate the ways in which you are meek. Our issue with Jesus' declaration is that we do not want to be meek.

Our aversion to meekness is so embedded in us that we are often blind to it. This is exemplified by Jerry Bridges' friend who, after listening to a series of messages on the Beatitudes given by Jerry, told him he had actually skipped the message on meekness. He wasn't interested in being meek.[1] Neither am I and neither are you.

There is a reason that we take issue with Jesus and his declaration. The reason is that we equate meekness with weakness. Matthew Henry observes: "Meekness is commonly despised

---

[1] Jerry Bridges recounts this story in *The Blessing of Humility* (Colorado Springs: NavPress, 2016), 27.

by the grandees of the age as cowardice."[2] Meek people are weak people, or at least that is the image we have conjured up in our mind. D. A. Carson captures this humorously by suggesting that we think a meek person could be knocked over by a hard slap with a wet noodle.[3] I am not sure if he is thinking of the foodstuff or the swimming aid. I prefer to picture the foodstuff; or to be more specific, someone teasing a long noodle out of a Pot Noodle, and then applying it ferociously to someone's face! It is a rather ludicrous image, but it paints the picture: meek people are weak people, or so we tell ourselves.

Not only do we equate meekness with weakness, but we also believe that weak people will be left empty-handed. The world is directed, owned and exploited by those who are strong. Only those who are willing to be bold, take the bull by the horns and assert their authority, will gain an inheritance worth talking about. The powerful will inherit the earth, or so we tell ourselves. In addition to taking issue with Jesus' call to be meek, therefore, we also take issue with his promise that the meek will inherit the earth. We behave as if it is a lie.

The belief that meekness equals weakness is a major misconception. Conducting our lives in a manner that implicates the veracity of Jesus' words carries serious implications. This discovery is the reason you hold this book in your hand. I am familiar with the Beatitudes, but it was not until I was asked to preach on the third Beatitude—blessed are the meek—that I was confronted with the reality I have described above. Without realising it I had taken issue with Jesus and his teachings. To be kind, I had completely ignored Jesus' declaration,

---

[2] Matthew Henry, *A Discourse on Meekness and Quietness of Spirit* (New York: American Tract Society, 1836), 48.

[3] D. A. Carson, *Sermon on the Mount: An Exposition of Matthew 5–7* (Carlisle: Paternoster Press, 2001), 22.

Introduction

"Blessed are the meek." To be honest, I had actively cultivated in my mind the lie that meek people are weak people. I cannot afford to be weak, so I do not need to be meek. Perhaps you have come to the same realisation in your own life and that is why you hold this book in your hand. Maybe it is a discovery that you are yet to make.

This book aims to combat the misconception that meekness is weakness. As I studied Scripture, I soon discovered that meek people are actually the strongest of people. In short, the Bible defines meekness as controlling our personal preferences in the present in full knowledge of our future blessings. The application of this truth has a bearing for us in true Christian discipleship, rightly aspiring to leadership and faithfully enduring suffering. In all of this, Jesus Christ is our exemplar—he leads the way.

Three sections comprise the vision of a truly meek Christianity. In part one we learn Messianic meekness directly from Jesus. He defines meekness by correcting the prevailing expectations concerning the Messiah (chapter 1), teaching his disciples how they are to live (chapter 2) and finally exhibiting it himself (chapter 3). In part two we are invited to adopt the Messiah's mindset as we explore Jesus' worldview based on Psalm 37. The third Beatitude is a direct quotation from Psalm 37:11. This Old Testament background will demonstrate the multiple injustices God's people face (chapter 4), the two destinies that await all people (chapter 5) and the one Judge who will eradicate all injustices and assign us our everlasting destiny (chapter 6). In part three we will catch a glimpse of the share of messianic majesty that awaits the meek. Both Psalm 37 and the third Beatitude promise an eternal inheritance for the meek (chapter 7) and, implicitly, a co-rulership with Jesus Christ (chapter 8).

By exploring meekness from a biblical perspective, we will quickly see that we do not take issue with Jesus when he declares, "Blessed are the meek, for they shall inherit the earth" (Matt. 5:5). Rather, Jesus takes issue with us.

Part One
Learning Messianic Meekness

1
A Tale of Two Kingdoms:
Constant Correction

It was the best of times, it was the worst of times, it was
the age of wisdom, it was the age of foolishness, it was the
epoch of belief, it was the epoch of incredulity, it was the
season of Light, it was the season of Darkness, it was the
spring of hope, it was the winter of despair, we had everything before us, we had nothing before us, we were all
going direct to Heaven, we were all going direct the other
way.[1]

So begins Charles Dickens' *A Tale of Two Cities*. Although
these famous lines introduce Dickens' historical novel set before and during the French Revolution they could serve as an
equally fitting introduction to the life and times of Jesus Christ.
The era during which Jesus of Nazareth walked the dusty roads
of the Near East was at once the best and worst of times.

The life and times of Jesus bring into greater focus not a tale
of two cities, but a tale of two kingdoms. One of the key features
of the ministry of Jesus was his focus on the kingdom of God
(or heaven).[2] It is the opening motif of his ministry (Matt. 4:17;
Mark 1:15), and throughout, Jesus repeatedly returns to this

---

[1] Charles Dickens, *A Tale of Two Cities*, Revised, Penguin Classics (London: Penguin, 2003), 5.

[2] The Gospel according to Matthew primarily uses the phrase kingdom of heaven
as opposed to kingdom of God. Despite some suggesting that these are two different
kingdoms, a careful reading of the context makes it abundantly clear that the kingdom
of God and the kingdom of Heaven are synonymous. It is likely that Matthew employs
the term "heaven" out of respect for his Jewish readers who may have retained some
qualms about saying God's name audibly.

same motif. Matthew helpfully records a series of parables that Jesus taught to explain further the kingdom of God (Matt. 13). In fact, preaching the good news of the kingdom of God was one of the purposes for the Father's sending Jesus (Luke 4:43; 8:1). Moreover, it was not enough for Jesus alone to preach the good news of the kingdom, and so he commands his disciples to join him in this venture (Luke 9:1-2, 57-62). This is something they do with great fervour and devotion after the ascension of Jesus and the outpouring of the Holy Spirit (Acts 1:3; 8:12; 19:8; 28:23, 30-31). This focus on the kingdom of God brings to the fore a tale of two kingdoms.

While there is widespread agreement that the kingdom of God forms a key motif in Jesus' preaching, it has proved a little more difficult to define what exactly Jesus means by the kingdom of God. There is no succinct definition recorded in the Gospels. Instead, Jesus introduces his explanations of the kingdom with the phrase: "the kingdom of God is like... ." Unfortunately, this has led to much debate. For our purposes it will be helpful to note one key feature of the kingdom of God as presented by Jesus. Vital to understanding the kingdom of God, as the Gospel authors record Jesus presenting it, is the realisation that it is not something we build. Rather, it is made for us. The kingdom of God is the experience of a new era in which a relationship with God is made possible through the saving work of Jesus Christ. More, it points forward to the permanent place in which this kingdom will be fully manifest: the new heavens and the new earth. The kingdom of God is the restoration of humanity's glad and willing submission to the perfect rule and reign of God which was lost through the rebellion of Adam and Eve in the Garden of Eden. This is achieved by the death of Jesus Christ on the cross and will be experienced in all its fullness in the new creation.

But I said that the life and times of Jesus Christ brought into focus a tale of two kingdoms, and so it does. The second kingdom is also known as the kingdom of God, but instead of being presented by Jesus it is a flawed view, presented by the Jews of his day. To be more specific it is a vision of the kingdom of God presented by particular groups of Jews. One group, known as the Essenes, withdrew from society, devoted themselves to the Law of God and awaited a supernatural army of heaven to arrive and establish the kingdom of God. They were ready to join the army of heaven and fight to establish the kingdom of God when the time came. The kingdom they envisioned, however, reflected the glory days of ancient Israel. The Essenes were awaiting a temporal kingdom located in a specific place.

Unlike the passive Essenes, a group known as the Zealots were true to their name. Although a poorly organised group, with very loose ties between different factions, they all had one common conviction: God would honour any military efforts to overthrow the kingdom of Rome and establish the kingdom of God. The Zealots actively attempted to do so through guerrilla warfare, assassination and stealing from the rich to give to the poor. In contrast to the Essenes, the Zealots were fighting for the kingdom now. They thought they could usher it in by their action.

Many Jews living in the first century did not belong to any particular group (such as Essenes, Zealots, Sadducees, or Pharisees). Even so, the hopes and dreams acted upon by these groups were the hopes and dreams hidden in the hearts of typical Jews. Thus, a tale of two kingdoms. The life and times of Jesus Christ was the best of times, the age of wisdom, the epoch of belief, the season of light, the spring of hope, everything the Jews had long awaited and taking us all to heaven, as Messianic expectation of the impending kingdom of God reached fever-pitch. Indeed, as Jesus himself proclaimed, the kingdom of God had arrived (Matt. 4:17; Mark 1:15; Luke 4:16–21). Yet the life and times of Jesus Christ was the worst of times, the age of foolishness, the epoch of incredulity, the season of darkness, the winter of despair, nothing at all like what the Jews had anticipated and taking us all the other way, as the Jews misplaced their Messianic expectation in something less than they should have. They did not understand the kingdom of God.

An Aversion to Meekness
What exactly has this tale of two kingdoms got to do with learning Messianic meekness? Everything. It demonstrates that our aversion to meekness is not a modern problem, it is an ancient one.

As we noted above, the key feature of Jesus' presentation of the kingdom of God was the realisation that it is not something we build. The Jews were eagerly anticipating the exact opposite. They expected the kingdom to be established in Jerusalem, and they expected to be participants in building the kingdom. The Jews hoped to do it themselves in the city they loved so dearly. Jesus established the heavenly Jerusalem as an expression of his kingdom; he had little interest in restoring its earthly counterpart. In addition to these mistaken ideas, the Jews knew they needed a charismatic leader. He was known as the Messiah. He had been promised by God. There were Scriptures that depicted the victory he would usher in when establishing the kingdom of God.

The Old Testament is replete with the hope and promise of a mighty, majestic Messiah. Israel's Scriptures assured their reader that there was one who would be victorious. The careful reader could hardly miss the majesty with which this Messiah is described. From beginning to end the Old Testament offers the confidence that a Messiah was coming to establish the kingdom of God.

If the kingdom of God is the restoration of humanity's glad and willing submission to the perfect rule and reign of God which was lost through the rebellion of Adam and Eve in the Garden of Eden, we might expect the first promise of the Messiah who would establish this kingdom to follow close on the heels of this disastrous disobedience in Genesis. And we are right. As God pronounces both judgement and salvation in Genesis 3 there is the remarkable promise that the woman's offspring will bruise the enemy's head (v. 15). There is a Messiah coming who will stamp on the head of the enemy. Yes, the enemy may strike the Messiah's heel, but that heel will crush the enemy's head.

The hope of this Messiah is given a royal hue in the historical books. This is particularly the case in 2 Samuel 7 as God promises to David, Israel's king *par excellence*, a son who will sit on his throne forever. A Davidic descendant will have a kingdom established forever by God. Matthew makes it unmistakably clear that in his mind Jesus is this king by including David in Jesus' genealogy (Matt. 1:1, 6, 17). The Messiah will be the king of an eternal kingdom—can this be anything other than the kingdom of God? The Jews were not stupid: they came up with the same answer as Matthew. This Jesus fits the mould of this Davidic Messiah.

Add to these two references the idyllic king portrayed in Israel's poetry. Psalm 72, for example, speaks of a king who in his righteousness provides for his kingdom (vv. 1–7). This king will also rule and reign so that his enemies will lick the dust as they fall down before him (vv. 8–11). This sounds like the type of Messiah who will crush the enemy's head and sit on his throne forever. In fact, Psalm 72 tells of a king's reign that will endure as long as the sun and moon shine (v. 5). This is a majestic Messiah.

When the prophets come to add some finer detail to this broad brushstroke image the message does not change. The prophet Isaiah promises the forlorn people of God that there is a Davidic descendant coming (11:1). He will be endowed with God's Spirit, which will enable him to be wise and powerful (v. 2). This wisdom and might will be executed with justice and righteousness (vv. 3–5). Inevitably, there will be peace (vv. 7–9), and so all nations will flock to him (v. 10). This is the kind of Messiah everyone wants: strong, upright, fair and victorious.

If these promises were a menu, we would be salivating. If these promises were a holiday brochure, we would be on the plane. If these promises were an online dating profile, we would have the wedding organised. If these promises were in an estate agent's window, we would be knocking on the bank manager's door. It is a magnificent and majestic character sketch of the Messiah. Picking up on this concept Owen Strachan writes: "The biblical metanarrative unfolds with speed and momentum, building the reader's expectation for the Messiah who will rescue God's people ... and set up a greater kingdom than any can imagine."[3] This is the type of Messiah that

---

[3] Owen Strachan, *Reenchanting Humanity: A Theology of Mankind* (Ross-shire: Mentor, 2019), 349.

the Jews of the first century were desiring. It was someone bearing this description that would inaugurate the kingdom of God.

Now, it must be admitted that the evidence is skewed somewhat. The Jews appeared to overlook the suffering of a royal servant described in Isaiah's "Servant Songs" (42:1-9; 49:1-7; 50:1-11; 52:13-53:12).[4] They neglected to include the suffering of the king in the book of Psalms. There the king is abandoned by God (Ps. 22) and betrayed by a friend (Ps. 69). The discipline promised by God for kings who transgressed his law (2 Sam. 7:14) was apparently ignored. Those awaiting the Messiah did not seem to fancy all of this perceived weakness. Someone who was willing to endure all of this, despite being a majestic king, could rightly be described as meek. That, however, is unappealing.

The Jews were looking for a mighty Messiah. No one wanted a meek Messiah. After all, they thought, only a mighty Messiah could overthrow the powerful Roman Empire and truly usher in the kingdom of God. We cannot condemn the Jews for this belief. Consider the leaders we seek out today: powerful, compelling, strong, unwavering, focused. Just like the Jews, we do not look for meekness. We are attracted to the assertive, the brash and the commanding. But the kingdom of God is different, and leadership within the kingdom is different. The stipulations for appointing leaders in the local church—which is a tangible manifestation of the kingdom of

---

[4] See my arguments at both a popular and academic level on reading Isaiah's 'Servant Songs' Christologically. S. D. Ellison, 'Who's the Mystery Guest in Isaiah's Servant Songs?', *The Gospel Coalition* (blog), 10 June 2020, https://www.thegospelcoalition.org/article/isaiahs-servant-songs; S. D. Ellison, ' "Man of Sorrows": A Christian Reading of Isaiah's Servant Songs,' *Semănătorul: The Journal of Ministry and Biblical Research* 1, no. 2 (2021): 83-96.

God yet to be experienced in its fullness—laid out by Paul in 1 Timothy 3 and Titus 1, make this clear. Commenting on those lists John Stott observes,

> A gift for leadership usually includes a forceful disposition. But pastors who have learned their leadership style from Jesus Christ will never ride rough-shod over other people's sensibilities. They will lead by example not by force, and by humble service not by self-assertion.[5]

The Jewish population in first century Jerusalem was awaiting an enigmatic figure who would win a following and lead them to victory. They were not looking for meek and mild; they were looking for mighty and wild. Do we look for anything different? All of us apparently possess an aversion to meekness.

A Mistaken Interpretation
When Jesus Christ began his public ministry, the Jews thought they had found whom they were waiting for. To be fair the accounts of Jesus' life and ministry recorded in the Gospels are rather remarkable. Who wouldn't be just a little impressed with someone who taught with authority, healed others and was ultimately confessed as the Messiah?

Matthew is keen to impress upon his reader the striking nature of Jesus' teaching. He does this in part by placing Jesus' teaching in five distinct blocks spread throughout his Gospel (5-7; 10; 13; 18; 23-25). The response to the first block of teaching reveals the impact that it had on its hearers: "And when Jesus had finished these sayings, the crowds were astonished at his teaching, for he was teaching them as one who had

---

[5] John R. W. Stott, *The Message of 1 Timothy and Titus*, Bible Speaks Today (Nottingham: Inter-Varsity Press, 2008), 177.

Tale of Two Kingdoms

authority, and not as their scribes" (7:28-29). The mighty, majestic Messiah would surely be able to teach with authority. How else could he gather an army around him to establish the kingdom of God?

In addition to teaching with authority, Jesus miraculously healed others. A snapshot of this is recorded for us in Matthew 8-9. In these two chapters Jesus heals a leper, a centurion's servant and Peter's mother-in-law; he proceeds to calm the sea, exorcise demons and heal a paralytic. Once more the response recorded by Matthew reveals the impact of these miracles. Jesus' own disciples marvelled, wondering who this Jesus really was (8:12). Those who knew the demon-possessed men before their exorcisms were terrified at the power of Jesus and begged him to leave their city (8:34). Those who saw the paralytic healed were afraid but gave glory to God (9:8). The mighty, majestic Messiah would surely be endued with a similar divine power. How else could he overthrow such a powerful opponent as the Roman Empire?

After witnessing his teaching and miracles, Jesus' disciples begin to realise just who he is. This realisation is revealed in Peter's confession. Jesus is aware of the gossip, and so he asks the disciples about it. "Who do people say I am?" Jesus asks (Matt. 16:13). There are a variety of answers given: John the Baptist, Elijah, Jeremiah, really any of the prophets (v. 14). Then Jesus turns the question on his disciples. "Very well then," replies Jesus, "who do you say that I am?" (v. 15). Peter speaks for the whole group with the declaration: "You are the Messiah" (v. 16). The confession is made! Someone has dared to utter the idea that this Jesus of Nazareth may actually be the one everyone has been waiting for.

Expectant Jews undoubtedly watched this man named Jesus with bated breath, high hopes and an ever-expanding excitement. They must have been open-mouthed as they listened to and discussed his teaching. They must have been wide-eyed as they heard reports of and witnessed his miracles. They must have murmured, "This could be him," as rumours of Peter's confession were passed on. To be fair, these diligent and expectant Jews could be forgiven for beginning to think: "This Jesus could be the one to lead an army and take back the Promised Land." But instead, Jesus pronounces: "Blessed are the meek, for they will inherit the earth" (Matt. 5:5). This is not the battling rally cry that the Jews had anticipated.

The Necessity for Constant Correction

I hope you have followed the logic throughout this chapter. The Jews, with hope burning painfully, were eagerly awaiting the Messiah. Their Scriptures promised him; their circumstances demanded him; the kingdom of God would only be established with his appearance. All of this expectation is swirling around in the first century, and then suddenly a man appears in the public eye. "The kingdom of God is here, repent and believe" (Mark 1:15). It is not simply a claim. Jesus backs up this declaration with astonishing teaching, terrifying miracles, and a band of brothers who after living with him day in, day out, confess him as the Messiah.

At this point we want to shout out, "Do it!" "Establish the kingdom." "Assert yourself." Everyone has been awaiting this mighty and victorious Messiah; everyone is desperate for him to yell "Charge!" They would follow him into battle without hesitation. Yet all that is heard is: "Blessed are the meek, for they shall inherit the earth" (Matt. 5:5). As Jerusalem twitches with expectancy, Jesus seems to press pause with this third Beatitude. Leon Morris notes that Jesus is teaching us: "Self-assertion is never a Christian virtue; rather, it is Christian to be busy in lowly service and refuse to engage in the conduct that merely advances one's personal aims."[6] This must be why Jesus urges those he heals to refrain from spreading the news (Matt. 9:30). He is seeking to calm this simmering hope.

The Jews were right, Jesus is the Messiah. It is just that their understanding of the Messiah and his kingdom was deficient. The kingdom they thought this Messiah was bringing was materially and militarily orientated. The Messiah was going to lead them to victory through violence. Conquest was the order of the day. But Jesus the Messiah dismisses this view with the third Beatitude. It is the meek, not the mighty, who will enter this kingdom and inherit the earth.[7]

Jesus is correcting the people of his own day, and his own people today. A biblical understanding of the kingdom of God must be holistic, fully-orbed. The kingdom of God is the restoration of humanity's glad and willing submission to the perfect rule and reign of God which was lost through the rebellion of Adam and Eve in the Garden of Eden. This undoubtedly incorporates victory won by the mighty Messiah, but it also includes the Messiah's heel being struck by the enemy. In meekness Jesus will embody the perceived weakness in the Old Testament's portrayal of the suffering Messiah.

All of this to say that we cannot understand meekness until we understand the kingdom of God. More, we cannot comprehend the Christian life until we grasp the nature of Christ's

---

[6] Leon Morris, *The Gospel According to Matthew*, Pillar New Testament Commentary (Leicester: Apollos, 1992), 98.

[7] This paragraph was aided by comments in D. Martyn Lloyd-Jones, *Studies in the Sermon on the Mount*, Reprint (Leicester: Inter-Varsity Press, 1984), 63–64.

kingdom. There is of course more to the kingdom than meekness, but there is not less. If the Messiah is meek, it follows that the Messiah's people must also be meek. If the true kingdom of God is established by a king of meekness, it follows that its citizens must also be marked by meekness. This is the constant correction that is ever necessary. As Matthew Henry lamented: "We are called Christians ... we name the name of the meek and lowly Jesus, but how few are actuated by his spirit, or conform to his example!"[8]

The correction Jesus offers, however, is not merely implicit. He speaks directly to this issue with the third Beatitude, and that is our focus in the next chapter.

---

[8] Henry, *A Discourse on Meekness and Quietness of Spirit*, 79.

2

A Familiar Sermon,
a High Calling

The Famous Sermon

Some people will forever have their name indelibly linked with a single sermon. The vivid illustration of settling for mud in the slums instead of a holiday on the beach will forever link C. S. Lewis with "The Weight of Glory" delivered in Oxford, England in 1941. The piercing image of handing a collection of seashells gathered in an extended retirement to the Creator God will forever link John Piper with "Don't Waste Your Life" delivered at the Passion conference in 2000. The title "Sinners in the Hands of an Angry God" need only be uttered, and most could supply the name Jonathan Edwards. He preached this sermon back in 1741, and yet Jonathan Edwards and "Sinners in the Hands of an Angry God" remain synonymous. Some people will forever have their name indelibly linked with a single sermon.

The same holds true for Jesus of Nazareth. When asked about the teaching of Jesus most could mention the Sermon on the Mount. This is undoubtedly Jesus' most famous sermon, and his name will forever be linked with it. In the last chapter Jesus' teaching was briefly mentioned. A distinctive aspect of Matthew's portrait of Jesus is Jesus as Teacher. In the Gospel according to Matthew the teaching of Jesus is divided into five blocks. Each of these blocks ends with a statement along the lines: "When Jesus finished these sayings" (Matt. 7:28; 11:1; 13:53; 19:1; 26:1). Matthew desires to present Jesus as the teacher *par excellence*. This is achieved in no small part by Matthew's recording the Sermon on the Mount in his Gospel. John Stott suggests that this is as close as we get to a manifesto from Jesus.[1]

This "manifesto" is a striking piece of teaching. Indeed, Leland Ryken proposes that "The Sermon on the Mount (Matt. 5-7) is the climax of Jesus' oratorical skill."[2] It is crammed full of pithy word pictures, such as "the salt of the earth" (5:13) or "the light of the world" (5:14). It is peppered with bold claims, such as Jesus fulfilling the law (5:17) or the repeated refrain "you have heard that it was said ... But I say to you" (5:21-22, 27-28, 31-32, 33-34, 38-39, 43-44). It mingles elevated ethical exhortations concerning generosity (6:1-4), fasting (6:16-18) and motivation (6:19-24) with the enormous encouragements of a heavenly Father who hears prayers (6:5-15) and provides necessities (6:25-34). It effectively employs humour, such as attempting to remove a speck from another's eye while having a plank sticking out of your own (7:1-5). It makes use of illustrations that stick, such as a tree being known by its fruit (7:16-20) or a house built on the sand (7:24-27). All of these dimensions make the Sermon on the Mount convicting, encouraging and memorable in equal measure. As John Stott observes: "It seems to present the quintessence of the teaching of Jesus. It makes goodness attractive. It shames our shabby performance. It engenders dreams of a better world."[3] It is a sermon worth having one's name indelibly linked to forever.

---

[1] John R. W. Stott, *The Message of the Sermon on the Mount*, Second Edition, Reprint, Bible Speaks Today (Nottingham: Inter-Varsity Press, 2008), 15.

[2] Leland Ryken, *Jesus the Hero: A Guided Literary Study of the Gospels*, Reading the Bible as Literature (Wooster: Weaver Book Company, 2016), 91.

[3] Stott, *The Message of the Sermon on the Mount*, 9.

Knowing Your Audience

A key element in whether a sermon will become famous is the audience. This is particularly apparent with Jonathan Edwards' sermon, "Sinners in the Hands of an Angry God." He had previously preached the sermon at his own church in Northampton with little or no discernible impact. Edwards then preached it at Enfield, a place that was becoming known for resisting God's work. It was there that the congregation responded with crying and weeping at the message he communicated to them. The commotion was substantial enough that Edwards had to stop preaching and the pastors present began to pray for the people in small groups. If that audience had not heard that sermon perhaps we would never have become aware of it. We must then ask, "Who were the first to hear the Sermon on the Mount?"

To answer that question, we must note how Matthew introduces the sermon. Matthew begins his portrayal of Jesus with an extended nativity narrative (chapters 1-2). He then details John the Baptist preaching in the wilderness and baptising Jesus (3). Jesus victoriously endures his temptation in the wilderness (4:1-11), and then begins his public ministry (4:12-17). Matthew presents the start of Jesus' public ministry in a compelling fashion. Almost a millennium prior to this moment the prophet Isaiah had promised the people of God that a son would be born and through him a light would be seen by the people of Zebulun and Naphtali (Isaiah 9:1-2). After noting that Jesus was in the territory of Zebulun and Naphtali (Matt. 4:13), Matthew quotes this prophecy of Isaiah (vv. 15-16). "From this time forward Jesus began to preach, saying, 'Repent, for the kingdom of heaven is at hand.'" (v. 17).

21

Given the feverish expectation surrounding the Old Testament promises of a coming one it is unsurprising that Jesus caused a commotion. This is initially apparent in Jesus' calling his first disciples (4:19) and their immediate obedience in following him (vv. 20, 22). Once Jesus begins teaching more publicly and healing diseases (v. 23) "his fame spread throughout all Syria … And great crowds followed him from Galilee and the Decapolis, and from Jerusalem and Judea, and from beyond the Jordan" (vv. 24–25). Jesus is the public attraction. Yet these crowds are not the audience for this famous sermon.

Before the Sermon on the Mount is delivered Jesus withdraws with his disciples (5:1). Having withdrawn with his disciples Jesus then teaches them (v. 2). The significance of this is that the Sermon on the Mount is delivered to those who are already followers of Jesus. This is important. The Sermon on the Mount is not a gospel message *per se*. The Sermon on the Mount is not a standard to be attained in order to gain acceptance. This famous sermon is not a gateway into the kingdom. Rather, it is a portrayal of those already in the kingdom. The Sermon on the Mount is a description of those who are already disciples. The first to hear the Sermon on the Mount are Jesus' first followers, and they are supposed to be seeing a reflection of themselves.

That first audience took this sermon seriously. It does however take some time, and the coming of the Holy Spirit (Acts 2), before it is fully implemented in the individual and corporate life of Jesus' followers. Nevertheless, this sermon shapes Jesus' disciples in a notable way. I wonder: does it continue to shape his disciples? This question will be fleshed out in more detail in this book with specific reference to meekness. But it is appropriate at this point to pause and consider our Christian character and witness—is our life shaped by the Sermon on the Mount?

As we reflect on our lives the Sermon on the Mount poses provoking questions. Does our life bring benefit to those around us like salt and light? Does our life exhibit self-control in anger, sex, promise-keeping and reacting to enemies? Is our life built on and around periods of prayer? Is our life pointed in the direction of God's kingdom and pressing onward in seeking it first? Jesus' manifesto would make it difficult for us to call ourselves disciples if our lives are not shaped by it.

The Basis of the Sermon

The Sermon on the Mount is a description of Jesus' disciples. This is true of the sermon's introduction, the Beatitudes. These nine blessings serve as an entry point for understanding the rest of Jesus' sermon. It is the launch pad for comprehending all that Jesus proceeds to set forth. The Beatitudes are the basis of the Sermon on the Mount. They portray the overall character of Jesus' followers before the specifics are outlined in the remainder of the sermon.

Moreover, the overall portrait of the follower of Jesus presented in the Beatitudes is a unity. The Beatitudes are not a buffet of Christian character traits to choose from. They are a unity, and together they describe the disciple. The corollary of this reality is that every one of Jesus' disciples is to exhibit the Beatitudes to an ever-increasing degree. This strongly suggests that the traits listed in the Beatitudes are not personality driven. Jesus could not demand that his disciples exhibit them if they were personality driven. Rather they are the work of the Holy Spirit in the life of the disciple. As Arthur W. Pink memorably puts it, they are "not constitutional, but gracious—a precious fruit of the Spirit's working."[4]

None of the Beatitudes is merely a tendency. Indeed, they cannot be if every Christian is to display all of them. The Beatitudes, and the Sermon on the Mount, depict the lifestyle of a disciple of Jesus. They describe a way of being. This is no less true of meekness, despite what the current cultural and Christian climate may suggest. It is to meekness we now turn.

Who Are the Blessed? Who Are the Meek?

I love Inca Kola: the "Golden Kola." It is a soft drink that originates in Peru. It is luminous yellow, undoubtedly bad for your teeth, and yet oh-so-good! It is very difficult to source outside Peru, and I am far too selfish with the stash that I bring home with me. As a result, I find it extremely difficult to convey to my family and friends how good this soft drink really is. I try my best to describe it. The taste is something similar to the Scottish soft drink Irn Bru, only with a stronger hint of bubblegum. But it also tastes different from Irn Bru. The best way to convey the delight of Inca Kola is to have someone taste it (as long as it isn't mine they are tasting). This illustrates the difficultly of attempting to convey all of the richness of the Greek terms that are translated as "blessed" and "meek."

In our *#blessed* world the term "blessed" now operates as a synonym for happiness. This is not the case in Scripture's use of the term. Happiness is much too subjective for what Jesus intends to communicate. Rather, in the Beatitudes "blessed" is a strong affirmation, yet it's also more. It is actually an

---

[4] Arthur W. Pink, *The Sermon on the Mount*, Reprint (Welwyn: Evangelical Press, 1977), 23. So too, Henry, *A Discourse on Meekness and Quietness of Spirit*, 93, who writes: 'Meekness is a grace of the Spirit's working, a garment of his preparing.'

objective declaration of divine favour. For Jesus, addressing his disciples, this declaration of divine favour leads to great joy. Therefore, while "blessed" includes the concept of being happy, it is not a mere synonym for happiness. As D. A. Carson explains, "Those who are blessed will generally be profoundly happy; but blessedness cannot be reduced to happiness."[5] When Jesus uses this term, he means more than mere happiness. He is pronouncing a deep joy found only in divine approval. As Matthew Henry notes, "We enjoy God when we have the evidences and assurances of his favour."[6] It is equally important to note the source of this joy: God. True happiness, or blessedness, is found only in God. Therefore, "We must also mortify the desire of the applause of men, as altogether inconsistent with our true happiness."[7]

Perhaps it would be more helpful to think of blessedness as a mood rather than a mere feeling. Joy in divine approval is deeper than a mere sentiment, it is a mindset and a heart-set — a mood. Elaborating this point Kevin Vanhoozer asserts:

Happiness is too shallow a term and fickle an emotion. Happiness is dependent on circumstances, and circumstances change. Often happiness is either inappropriate or inauthentic in our in-between times, marked by finitude and suffering. By way of contrast, resurrection joy is a *mood*, a way of being attuned to the world — when one knows that the world includes an empty tomb. Happiness is a surface phenomenon, but for those who

---

[5] Carson, *Sermon on the Mount*, 18.
[6] Henry, *A Discourse on Meekness and Quietness of Spirit*, 56.
[7] Henry, 147.

through faith enjoy being-in-Christ, joy resides in the depths of their being.[8]

The objective declaration of divine favour announced in the Beatitudes is not hostage to changing circumstances. It is a deep disposition, enjoyed only by those who have experienced Christ. Indeed, pressing further into this concept it transpires that the divine approval that results in a mood of transcendent joy has the happy consequence of seeing the "blessed" flourish.

Jesus teaches that this divine approval that results in a deep joy will be experienced by those who are meek. The Greek term translated as "meek" in the Beatitudes possesses numerous shades of meaning. Indeed, trying to describe those shades is similar to trying to describe Inca Kola. Nevertheless, we can note at least four concepts present in the Greek term translated "meek." First, this term carries the idea of gentleness. It describes the person who is free from malice and vengefulness. The meek person is temperate. Second, this gentleness is a choice. The meek person is active in his meekness. It is not simply a case of being shy or introverted. To be meek demands that an individual is self-effacing. As Martin Lloyd-Jones put it: "The man who is truly meek is the one who is amazed that God and man can think of him as well as they do and treat him as well as they do."[9] Third, the self-effacing nature implies a measure of self-control. Those who are meek are not so simply because they are incapable of being otherwise. Rather, they control themselves by choosing to be meek. We could say that "Meekness is a controlled desire to see other's interests

---

[8] Kevin J. Vanhoozer and Owen Strachan, *The Pastor as Public Theologian: Reclaiming a Lost Vision* (Grand Rapids: Baker Academic, 2015), 107.

[9] Lloyd-Jones, *Studies in the Sermon on the Mount*, 69.

advance ahead of one's own."[10] Alternatively, Lloyd-Jones summarises meekness as our ability "to leave everything— ourselves, our rights, our cause, our whole future—in the hands of God, and especially so if we feel we are suffering unjustly."[11] Fourth, and finally, the meek person is strong. The word is employed to describe someone who is strong enough to defer to others. Often only weak people foist their opinions and desires on others. The strong are able to stand back and defer to others.

As a working definition, to be filled out in the next chapter, we could say that meekness is a knowledge of one's standing before God which provides an inner strength enabling one to act for the benefit of others, even at their own expense. The meek, then, are those whose attitude and behaviour is driven by the understanding that they are disciples. In comprehending the privileges enjoyed as disciples the meek are able to refrain from promoting themselves and their preferences. The meek restrain their own desires in order to serve others. Commenting on the use of the same Greek term in Titus 3:2, William Mounce suggests that meekness "denotes a humility, a courtesy, a consideration of others without being servile."[12] As the Apostle Paul would later put it, the meek "count others as more significant" (Phil. 2:3). This is not mere humility, however. It is humility equipped with gentleness, and always seeking the good of another.

[10] Carson, *Sermon on the Mount*, 23.
[11] Lloyd-Jones, *Studies in the Sermon on the Mount*, 70.
[12] William D. Mounce, *Pastoral Epistles*, Word Biblical Commentary 46 (Grand Rapids: Zondervan, 2016), 445.

A High Calling

The remarkable element in all of this careful definition of terms is that Jesus does not force obedience in this arena. Jesus does not override our hardwiring. Rather, through the pronouncement of the Beatitudes and the delivery of the Sermon on the Mount, Jesus invites his followers willingly to glorify their Saviour.

A parent, guardian, or teacher will appreciate the sense of satisfaction when a child does the right thing of their own volition. Walking a child step-by-step through an apology to a sibling or classmate may be necessary, and a good teaching opportunity, but it is rarely satisfying. Watching a child initiate an apology because they comprehend the situation is a delight. This depicts the opportunity we have to embrace our high calling. We can wrestle against it, or we can willingly yield. As Jesus pronounces "Blessed are the Meek" we have the occasion willingly to yield.

This is a high calling. We are not mere puppets to be manipulated. We are not pre-programmed robots. As disciples of Jesus Christ we are thinking, acting beings. In that, Jesus is calling us to use our heads and our hearts. He desires us to employ our intelligence and our will. The invitation in the Beatitudes is to choose to live differently because we are disciples. This is remarkable. The Creator and Sustainer of the entire cosmos compels us through invitation willingly to look to the interests of others.[13] Jesus reminds us that as disciples our calling is to embrace meekness readily. If we do so we have the privilege of bringing delight to our Lord.

---

[13] Likewise, Strachan, *Reenchanting Humanity*, 37, writes: 'We have been constituted by God, given minds and passionate hearts and bodies, and the Lord's good will for us is that we dedicate all our faculties and energies to living praise of him.'

It should stun us that the all-powerful and all-knowing One should invite us to obedience. Given that in his sovereignty he could make us obedient and in his omniscience, he knows our inevitable failure, it is remarkable that God desires our cooperation in living the kingdom life. The almighty God, our Lord and Saviour, awaits our response to his invitation. And by the power of his Spirit, we are able.

We are not simply left to our own devices, however. God himself empowers us for obedience by presencing himself in us—God the Spirit indwells and equips us for living the Christian life. In addition to God at work in us through the Spirit, we also see Jesus demonstrate meekness for us. It is to his example that we turn next.

3
The Meek Messiah

The Copy Without Blot

As Paul begins to close his letter to the church in Philippi, he challenges them with these words "Finally, brothers, whatever is true, whatever is honourable, whatever is just, whatever is pure, whatever is lovely, whatever is commendable, if there is any excellence, if there is anything worthy of praise, think about these things" (Phil. 4:8).

Paul's desire is for the Christians in Philippi to permit truth and beauty to shape their attitudes. True worship can ever only be the result of minds filled with and renewed by an attractive reality (Rom. 12:2) and affections enthused by the grace of God (Phil. 4:9).

If we look for a personification of what is true, honourable, just, pure, lovely, commendable, excellent and praiseworthy there is one who stands out: Jesus Christ. Jesus is the example above all others. Paul's list of attributes is pre-eminently displayed in the life of Jesus. He exemplifies them perfectly. This reality makes it wise to heed the exhortation to look to Jesus (Heb. 12:2). Looking to Jesus is our aim in this chapter as we learn that Jesus not only corrects our deliberation about and definition of meekness, but he also proceeds to demonstrate meekness. We are about to meet the meek Messiah.[1]

Attempting to illustrate true meekness, Matthew Henry points us towards the patterns of meekness found in Scripture.

---

[1] Such a meeting should not leave us unchanged. As Strachan, 258, asserts: 'Meeting the Messiah through repentant faith corrects the messianic expectations of the modern world.'

The familiar heroes of the faith are mentioned: Abraham, Moses, David and Paul. Eventually, Henry arrives at Jesus. He writes: "But, after all, our Lord Jesus was the great pattern of meekness and quietness of spirit; all the rest had their spots, but here is the copy without a blot."[2] While other people's attempts at meekness might look like a dog-eared newspaper, turning yellow and covered in ink and coffee stains, Jesus' meekness looks like a crisp, blindingly white page hosting an enthralling message, produced by beautiful penmanship and with no hint of a smudge. The meek Messiah is the copy without blot.

Matthew is keen to communicate this fact to the readers of his Gospel. On two occasions he uses the same Greek term from the third Beatitude in relation to Jesus (11:29; 21:5). Indeed, it does not appear to be Matthew's understanding alone. In the first instance the term is found on the lips of Jesus himself; in the second instance it is found on the lips of the prophet Zechariah.

Meekness in Open Arms
We have already considered the feverish expectation that was part and parcel of Jewish thinking in Jesus' day (see chapter 1). While Jesus appeared to tick all the messianic boxes, not everyone was convinced. Jesus may have taught in a most remarkable manner (Matt. 7:28-29) and performed the most marvellous miracles (9:33), but Matthew ensures that his readers realise that Jesus also faced fierce opposition. The aligning of Jesus with the expected Jewish messiah certainly wasn't universal.

---

[2] Henry, *A Discourse on Meekness and Quietness of Spirit*, 109.

At first this opposition is implicit. It seems that while the religious leaders criticised John the Baptist for fasting, suggesting he was demon-possessed (Matt. 11:18), they criticised Jesus for feasting, suggesting he was a glutton, drunkard and sinner (v. 19). Hostility towards Jesus is then explicitly expressed by a refusal to repent (vv. 20-24). In Matthew 12 we read of the Pharisees accusing Jesus of breaking the law (vv. 1-14), serving the Devil (v. 24) and failing to substantiate his claims (v. 38). The opposition is now explicit, even if there is room for it to escalate.

Nestled in the middle of the rising antagonism in Matthew 11 and 12 is the revelation of the Saviour's heart for spent sinners.[3] Jesus declares "Come to me, all who labour and are heavy laden, and I will give you rest. Take my yoke upon you, and learn from me, for I am gentle [meek] and lowly in heart, and you will find rest for your souls. For my yoke is easy, and my burden is light" (Matt. 11:28-30).

Jesus declares that he is gentle and lowly, or meek and humble. The Greek word translated as gentle here is in fact the same Greek word translated as meek in the third Beatitude. It is an astonishing statement. Just prior to this statement Jesus asserts his power and sovereignty; he makes it clear that he possesses a privileged position with the Father (v. 27). Yet this position of strength is not exploited in the face of opposition. As Dane Ortlund explains: "Jesus is not trigger happy. Not harsh, reactionary, easily exasperated. He is the most understanding person in the universe. The posture most natural to him is not a pointed finger but open arms."[4] Despite his

---

[3] For more on this being the heart of Jesus Christ see, Dane C. Ortlund, *Gentle and Lowly: The Heart of Christ for Sinners and Sufferers* (Wheaton: Crossway, 2020).

[4] Ortlund, 19.

extraordinary power, he does not attack those attacking him. Instead, Jesus welcomes with open arms those who approach him.

This is meekness. The perfect demonstration of what it is to be strong enough to defer to others at the expense of self. As Jesus surveys the crowd, he sees those who are striving with all their energy for something they will never achieve. As he surveys the lost sheep of Israel, he sees those who are pressed down under the weight of Pharisaic law in the hope of pleasing God. As he peers beyond the surface, he sees still others who are seething with rage at the audacity of his words. Rather than demanding that those antagonistic towards him bow down in recognition of who he truly is, Jesus defers to the weakest in the crowd; because he is meek, he invites those who are striving and weighed down to find rest in him. Jesus demonstrates his meekness with open arms.

The best teachers do not only tell their students what to do, they show their students what to do. The most powerful examples of virtue are those who live it. This is one of the reasons that Jesus is perhaps the most potent moral example ever, even for those who do not profess to be Christians. Truly he forgave his bitterest enemies (Luke 23:34), and so his call to follow suit rings with authority (Matt. 5:43–48; 18:35). It is difficult to ignore this level of commitment.

During the Reformation a similar level of commitment was on display. Many went to their death for living what they taught. Others brought life by living what they taught. The marriage between Martin Luther the monk and Katharina von Bora the nun is one such example. In this single act they both risked death and granted life. Luther declared that marriage, family and children were not lesser vocations as the medieval clergy had long taught. He refused to see celibacy as a superior state for the churchman. As far as he could see, the Scriptures contained no such teaching. However, Luther did not simply teach this; he lived it. In a scandalous marriage for the sixteenth century, the monk married the nun. As one historian observes, "What Luther taught he now lived as well."[5] And so it was with Jesus: what he taught he also lived. Jesus is the meek Messiah.

Meekness in Kingship

It is instructive to note that each Gospel author arranges his material in a particular sequence in order to make particular points. This is part of the reason why the Gospels do not all follow an identical order. Therefore, we must not overlook the fact that Matthew precedes Jesus' triumphal entry (21:1–11) with an account of Jesus giving blind men sight (20:29–34). Matthew is keen that his readers have at the forefront of their minds the concept of eyes being opened as they read Jesus' revelation of himself as the "the very King of meekness."[6] Matthew is about to reiterate that Jesus is the meek Messiah, and he does not want his readers to miss it.

Earlier in Matthew Jesus urged his followers not to proclaim his messiahship (16:20; 17:9). Now, however, Jesus is found actively and deliberately making plans to reveal who he is:

Now when they drew near to Jerusalem and came to Bethphage, to the Mount of Olives, then Jesus sent two

---

[5] Heiko A. Oberman, *Luther: Man between God and the Devil*, trans. Eileen Walliser-Schwarzbart, English Paperback (London: Yale University Press, 2006), 284. For more on how the Reformation impacted various aspects of life, see S. D. Ellison, *Five: The Solas of the Reformation* (Lansvale: Tulip Publishing, 2020), 71–87.

[6] Pink, *The Sermon on the Mount*, 23.

disciples, saying to them, "Go into the village in front of you, and immediately you will find a donkey tied, and a colt with her. Untie them and bring them to me. If anyone says anything to you, you shall say, 'The Lord needs them,' and he will send them at once." (21:1-3)

These verses make it clear that there has been deliberate planning on Jesus' part. Jesus is fully aware that the time has come to reveal himself as Messiah. Some of this kind of thinking inevitably had been leaked already, but now Jesus himself was going to make the claim.

According to Matthew, Jesus' actions are the fulfilment of prophecy (21:4). The Old Testament prophet Zechariah foretold that God would set foot on the Mount of Olives and, after winning victory over all enemies, return to Jerusalem (14:4). In Matthew 21:1 we are told that Jesus is standing on the Mount of Olives. Throughout the Gospel he has repeatedly refuted his enemies. And now, this Jesus rides into Jerusalem on a donkey. Matthew points out that this is the fulfilment of Zechariah 9:9 (Matt. 21:5).

Matthew 21 depicts a poignant scene. The declaration is the that the long-awaited Messiah-King has arrived. The scenes are jubilant (vv. 8-9). The explanation, offered by quoting Zechariah, is that this individual is an individual of meekness. The prophet is clear. The emphasis in the quotation from Zechariah is meekness. Jesus is revealing he is the long-awaited Messiah-King that Israel has been anticipating. However, Jesus' messianic reign will be of a very different nature to that which is expected. The people desired a valiant king riding into occupied Jerusalem on a white stallion ready to drive out the Romans. The Messiah arrives on a donkey in the city in which he will die. Donkeys were indeed a royal mount, but generally used by kings seeking peace. Rather than riding a beast for battle, Jesus trundles in on a creature of peace. In meekness the king enters his own city with a message of peace for the occupying forces. Here is Jesus' meekness in kingship. Just as Jesus announced his meekness to the crowds in Matthew 11, so now Jesus demonstrates his meekness to the crowds in Matthew 21. Just as Jesus invited the weak and weary to come to him in Matthew 11, so now Jesus is resolved to secure their acceptance when they come. The Messiah is meek.

Given Jesus' meekness as demonstrated in revealing his heart in Matthew 11 and his meekness in revealing his messianic kingship in Matthew 21, it follows that citizens of his kingdom should exhibit the same characteristics. This is true for all Christians, but it is particularly pertinent to Christian leadership; especially given Jesus is revealing how he as king leads.

For too long and too often Christian visions of leadership have been shaped by the culture and context in which they are formed. Sometimes this has yielded biblical aspects of leadership. Far too often it results in a twisted vision of Christian leadership. Christian leaders are subjects in the kingdom of God. All subjects must follow the lead of the king of the kingdom: the meek Messiah. We must know our king and emulate our king. We should be people of meekness. Our world is full of people jostling for position, power, pride and recognition. Sadly, Christian behaviour is frequently little different—whether inside the church or outside the church, we are commonly found fighting for position, power, prestige and recognition. But this is not who Jesus is. It is not who we should be.[7]

---

[7] For further reflection on this theme, see S. D. Ellison, 'This Is Meekness', *For The Church* (blog), 18 March 2022, https://ftc.co/resource-library/blog-entries/this-is-meekness.

Intensely Passionate Meekness

Meekness is not weakness, however. As Warren Wiersbe explains, "Meekness is not weakness. It is power under control."[8] This we have asserted above, and in the very next section of Matthew's Gospel it is confirmed. Jesus Christ, the meek Messiah, is able to be angry and yet remain sinless. Moreover, he is not simply angry; Jesus acts on his anger, overthrowing tables and chasing people away from the temple because they are profaning this sacred space (Matt. 21:12–13).

The more I ponder this the more incredible it becomes. How can the one who embodies meekness in perfection act in such a way? It seems that the answer to this question resides in the motivation for such anger and action. As John Piper observes, "Meekness does not mean the absence of passion and conviction and even indignation for the glory of God."[9] Jesus acts for the glory of God. His anger is due to the defaming of God's reputation by the sellers in the temple. His actions work towards re-establishing the glory of God. Jesus' intense passion in no way diminishes his meekness.

Is it possible for us to demonstrate such passion for the glory of God and yet remain meek? I suggest that it is. Given our fallen nature it is difficult. The purity of our motivation must always be assessed carefully. At times, however, it is both right and necessary to confront boldly those who are attempting to rob God of his glory. Aristotle offers some helpful advice in thinking along these lines: "The one who is truly meek is the one who becomes angry on the right grounds against the right person in the right manner at the right moment and for the

---

[8] Warren W. Wiersbe, *Be Rich: Gaining the Things That Money Can't Buy (NT Commentary: Ephesians)*, Second Edition (Colorado Springs: David C. Cook, 2009), 107.

[9] John Piper, 'Blessed Are the Meek', Desiring God, accessed 17 June 2020, https://www.desiringgod.org/messages/blessed-are-the-meek.

right length of time."[10] Sage advice. It is also enlightening advice as it illuminates the difficulty in remaining meek and yet demonstrating exuberant passion. In fact, this further underlines an important observation concerning meekness: its inner strength. Consider the level of self-control necessary to be angry on the right grounds, against the right person, in the right way, at the right time and for the right duration.

The cleansing of the temple is an exercise of intensely passionate meekness. As we have continued to add layer upon layer in our quest to learn messianic meekness, we have reached a vital point. Jesus Christ constantly corrected the mistaken version of messiah that the Jews were expecting; he explicitly taught that his followers must be meek, living a life distinct from those around them; he demonstrated the life of meekness in himself. Nonetheless, this Jesus was not reclusive and soporific; he was not feeble and fearful; he was not weak. Quite the opposite, Jesus Christ was bold, confrontational, engaging and zealous. Yet without impinging on his meekness.

Follow Me

The meek Messiah is the copy without blot, the superlative example of meekness. The importance of this realisation is found in the revelation that our Saviour does not call us to do anything he was not himself willing to do. Let that sink in. Every command that Jesus issues is one that he obeys. Jesus is not a "Do as I say" teacher, he is a "Follow me" teacher. We do not simply obey the commands he issues; we follow his example.

I write this section in the wake of Covid-19 and as the United Kingdom tentatively steps out of lockdown. In recent

---

[10] As in Kenneth E. Bailey, *Jesus Through Middle Eastern Eyes: Cultural Studies in the Gospels* (London: SPCK, 2008), 73.

weeks our governments have repeatedly urged us to stay at home and save lives. Much of the population has heeded the repeated warnings. Many have made severe sacrifices to follow government guidelines and regulations. In some instances, however, the very people creating and delivering these guidelines have completely disregarded them. In Scotland the Chief Medical Officer visited a second home two weekends in a row after appearing on television to urge everyone else to stay at home. She was saying one thing but doing another. In England a key government advisor on Coronavirus not only broke the lockdown rules but did so to engage in an extra-marital affair. This was followed by the Prime Minister's Chief Advisor also flouting the regulations. Indeed, the Prime Minister at the time is himself guilty of breaking the rules he made. All of these people said one thing but did another. Each of these individuals told us to behave in one way, but they behaved according to an alternative standard. The result? The general population began to feel liberation to ignore the regulations. There is no impetus to heed the advice if the very people giving it are refusing to live by it themselves.

Jesus is the antithesis of such hypocrisy. His perfect obedience to his own commands offers us two points of reflection on messianic meekness. First, Jesus' meekness offers us encouragement. Jesus is a man of integrity. He is not calling his disciples to follow his rhetoric, rather he is calling his disciples to follow his life. Jesus' call to follow him is an invitation to watch him closely and emulate what we witness. This should be an encouragement to us. The weight of this is immense. God in the flesh is not only the firstborn in resurrection, he is the firstborn in true discipleship. Jesus is the firstborn in meekness. Look to him.

Second, even though Jesus is God in the flesh he accomplishes the high calling of meekness in the same way we are to accomplish it. Jesus lives meekly in the flesh by the power of the Spirit. Jesus is not cheating. He does not pull out the "God card" and skip the harsh reality of living life as a human. Jesus lived his life with the same divine resources as his followers do. Bruce Ware captures this helpfully:

> The only way to make sense, then, of the fact that Jesus came in the power of the Spirit is to understand that he lived his life fundamentally as a man, and as such, he relied on the Spirit to provide the power, grace, knowledge, wisdom, direction, and enablement he needed, moment by moment and day by day, to fulfil the mission the Father sent him to accomplish ... He lived his life as one of us. He accepted the limitations of his humanity and relied upon the guidance the Father would give him and the power the Spirit would provide him to live day by day in perfect obedience to the Father.[11]

Jesus achieves the high calling of meekness in exactly the same way we are to achieve it: by employing our wills to obey the Father in the power of the Spirit. We look to him and we follow him.

It is striking that in the very act of not calling us to do anything he was not willing to do himself, Jesus exhibits the very meekness that he is seeking in his followers. Encouragingly, he walked the talk. He has demonstrated that our high calling is achievable in the flesh and by the power of the Spirit. Jesus declares with all authority, "Follow me." Our prayer must

[11] Bruce A. Ware, *The Man Christ Jesus: Theological Reflections on the Humanity of Christ* (Wheaton: Crossway, 2012), 34, 43.

always be, "Help me to walk as Jesus walked, my only Saviour and perfect model ... Let my happy place be amongst the poor in spirit, my delight the gentle ranks of the meek. Let me always esteem others better than myself."[12]

Messianic Meekness: A Summary

In this first part of the book, we have been learning Messianic meekness. To begin with we observed in the first chapter that meekness cannot be correctly understood without an adequate comprehension of the kingdom of God. The kingdom is an exhibition in meekness. It is a subversive reality. Jesus' constant correction is no less necessary today—especially with respect to the types of leaders to whom we are naturally attracted. In our second chapter we explored the context in which the call to meekness is issued, Jesus' most famous sermon—the Sermon on the Mount. By doing so we developed our definition of meekness. Meekness is a knowledge of one's standing before God which provides an inner strength enabling one to act for the benefit of others, even at one's own expense. It was then noted that this is not something God forces us to do; rather he invites us to do it. The third chapter fleshed out this definition by witnessing the meek Messiah. Jesus demonstrates what it means to be meek. As the Son of God, Jesus is strong enough to choose to overlook opposition for the benefit of the weary and burdened at the expense of defending himself. As the Messianic-King, Jesus is strong enough to refuse to fulfil the temporal hopes of the Jews by riding on a donkey into Jerusalem for the benefit of the whole world at the expense of his life.

The calling to be meek is a call to recognise our standing before God in order to provide an inner strength to enable us

---

[12] Taken from the prayer "Christlikeness" in The Valley of Vision.

to act for the benefit of others, even at our own expense. Jesus is our perfect example. Edmund Clowney illustrates Jesus' meekness by drawing attention to his washing the disciples' feet: "Jesus took the towel, knowing who he was, from where he had come, and where he was going. Secure in that knowledge, he was untouched by the defensiveness of insecure pride."[13] If the call for us as disciples is to follow Jesus' pattern, the natural question is, "How?" After learning what meekness is, how do we live it in our life? That is what part two is about: adopting the Messiah's mindset.

---

[13] Edmund P. Clowney, *The Church*, Contours of Christian Theology (Downers Grove: Inter-Varsity Press, 1995), 62.

Part Two:
Adopting the Messiah's Mindset

4

Multiple Injustices:
The Christian's Constant Companion

A Question of Mindset

Insight into another's mindset is fascinating. Love him or loathe him, Sir Alex Ferguson is an individual whose mindset many people are keen to glimpse. He is the most successful British football manager ever, winning 38 trophies in a 27-year spell as manager of Manchester United. More remarkable than the trophy haul is the fact that he altered the entire culture of the club, transforming them from mid-table mediocrity to serial winners. He did this by instilling a new mindset—a mindset driven by character and commitment. His own mindset. Ferguson was interested in more than simply a player's talent. He wanted to know the player's character, upbringing and ambition, often choosing to meet the parents of younger players.

Sadly, in May 2013, Sir Alex Ferguson announced the news every Manchester United fan had dreaded: he was retiring from football management. Having grown up in working-class Scotland, Govan in Glasgow to be exact, Ferguson was no stranger to long hours of hard work. He carried this attitude into his professional managerial career and instilled it in his players. Manchester United as a football club was driven to use every second of time and every ounce of ability and every penny in the bank to attain perfection.

How does someone who lived in such an environment for so long adapt to retirement? One day every waking moment is spent watching, thinking, reading and organising football. The next day the diary is blank. How does someone like that ensure that each day is productive? After all, with Ferguson's current bank balance there is no need to keep working (I assume).

An insight into Sir Alex Ferguson's retirement mindset is offered at the end of his book, *Leading*. Initially he explains part of the challenge in retirement: "In 2013, for the first time in my life, my most pressing need, as I relaxed by the Mediterranean, was to beat my brother-in-law, John Robertson, at Kaluki." But Ferguson's retirement was far more active than this. He then proceeds to explain how he stayed active and productive in retirement: "I keep remembering a short piece of advice about tomorrow that I was given before I retired. It was, 'Don't put your slippers on.' The line has stuck with me. It's why I put my shoes on right after breakfast."[1] A fiercely active retiree may have fostered that mindset by the simple act of putting on his shoes after eating his breakfast.

In part one of this book, we have engaged with Jesus directly on the issue of meekness. Just as I watched in joy and wonder at Sir Alex Ferguson leading Manchester United to triumph after triumph, so we have witnessed as Jesus, with joy and amazement, demonstrates true meekness again and again. In part two of this book, we are turning our attention to Jesus' mindset. Our hope is to catch a glimpse of the mindset that undergirded the meekness Jesus both taught and exemplified. Just as glimpsing Ferguson's mindset offers a compelling view of how he thinks, so too with Jesus. In comprehending the capacity for and devotion to meekness that Jesus displayed, it is all a question of mindset. The way in which we glimpse Jesus' mindset is by reading the Bible Jesus read—exploring the Old

---

[1] Alex Ferguson, *Leading* (London: Hodder and Stoughton, 2016), 339, 343.

Testament. More specifically, our attention will be directed almost exclusively to Psalm 37.

Psalm 37

Psalm 37 has not been chosen at random. A careful reading of the psalm soon reveals that this is the passage in which Jesus found inspiration for both living and teaching the third Beatitude. In fact, the third Beatitude is almost a direct quotation of Psalm 37:11:

> But the meek shall inherit the land and delight themselves in abundant peace. (Ps. 37:11)

> Blessed are the meek, for they shall inherit the earth. (Matt. 5:5)

In recognising this we find the key to gaining an insight into the Messiah's mindset: understanding the Old Testament. In turn, familiarity with this Old Testament passage in particular aids a true understanding of the third Beatitude. Derek Kidner makes explicit the importance of Psalm 37 in understanding Matthew 5:5 by asserting: "There is no finer exposition of the third beatitude than this psalm."[2] For this reason we turn our attention to the Old Testament.

It is important to pause at this point and note the significance of this fact. For much too long far too many Christians have neglected the Old Testament. Apart from a favourite "inspirational" verse or two, large stretches of the Old Testament are foreign territory for Christians. This is scandalous. In the first instance this betrays a poor understanding of the concept

---

[2] Derek Kidner, *Psalms 1-72*, Tyndale Old Testament Commentaries 15 (Nottingham: Inter-Varsity Press Academic, 2008), 166.

of canon. The Christian Scriptures constitute both the Old and New Testaments—the Christian's Bible is not merely the New Testament. The Christian canon consists of sixty-six books—Genesis to Revelation. The reality that some of Jesus' most famous and memorable teaching is based so heavily on the Old Testament should be a personal enlightenment in recognising the importance of the Old Testament for the Christian. Indeed, when we consider that the Apostles in Acts preached the gospel from the Old Testament alone, we begin to realise that the church was founded on the message of the books of the Bible often neglected by Christians today. J. Gresham Machen likewise remarks: "The Old Testament Scriptures testified of Christ, and the first preachers made full use of the Scripture testimony."[3] Second, in order to explore the full riches of the New Testament we must be familiar with the Old Testament which undergirds so much of it. To appreciate the full weight of the third Beatitude we need to understand Psalm 37. The opposite is also true: to appreciate the true depth of Psalm 37 we must see its use in the New Testament. As readers permit the content of the first thirty-nine books to inform their reading of the last twenty-seven, and vice versa, a more vibrant message emerges from the pages of Scripture. All of this to say: Christian, get to know your Old Testament. In doing so your comprehension of the Scriptures, the gospel they proclaim and the Saviour they reveal will become much richer.

My hope is that this and the next two chapters will demonstrate how a better understanding of the Old Testament helps us see the beautiful depth of the New Testament. And as we

---

[3] J. Gresham Machen, *The New Testament: An Introduction to Its Literature and History* (Edinburgh: Banner of Truth, 1976), 312.

focus on Psalm 37 there is one uncomfortable reality that we are immediately confronted with: injustice.

The Revulsion of Injustice

Nothing excites emotion like injustice, whether perceived or real. The injustice that most frequently exercises my emotions on a regular basis is other drivers breaking the law. While I attempt to be a submissive citizen living a quiet and godly life in my car, others disregard the laws about using a mobile phone, not wearing a seatbelt, breaking the speed limit and all without retribution. Worse, if I pay careful attention, the culprit always looks richer than I, drives a nicer car and is using the latest iPhone. Meanwhile, I get pulled over by the police for no apparent reason. In fact, once I was breathalysed even though the only drink I had consumed was copious amounts of tea! It is the injustice that stings.

Of course, my frivolous experience of a minor injustice is a mere shadow of the injustices that plague the globe. The wilful, and largely legal, murder of unborn children. The exploitation of women, both young and older, for selfish sexual satisfaction. The institutional racism that either punishes or rewards on the inexplicable basis of skin colour. The neglect of orphaned children, homeless teenagers, or mature refugees. The silent extinguishing of the aged and debilitated by euthanasia in the name of mercy. God's good creation is stained throughout with injustice.

Psalm 37 confronts its reader with the reality of injustice from the outset and continues to do so repeatedly. As Willem VanGemeren points out, "At issue is the power, greed, and

prosperity of the wicked and the suffering of the righteous."[4]
More simply, at issue is injustice. Psalm 37's depiction of this
injustice repels us, or at least it should. Immediately the reader
encounters evildoers and wrongdoers (Ps. 37:1). The Psalmist
acknowledges that although these individuals are engaged in
wilfully wicked activities, they often appear to prosper (vv. 7,
35). In fact, regularly the wicked directly target the righteous
with seething hatred (v. 12), and thus prosper at the expense of
those who are dutiful in their righteousness. Mimicking the in-
stinctive hunters of the natural world, those who are evil or delight in wrong target the weak and helpless (v. 14)—picking off
the stragglers. All of this deceitful behaviour brings about an
abundance that should belong only to the righteous (vv. 16, 21).
Cunning plans with devastating aims are concocted by the evil
(v. 32). Throughout Psalm 37 the psalmist describes evildoers
and wrongdoers who, at the apparent expense of the righteous,
frequently appear to succeed in all their evil intentions. Injustice seems to triumph.

In accord with our experience, Psalm 37 affirms that injustice pervades, and often prevails in, our world. As a consequence of the fall injustice is the Christian's constant companion. The ravages of sin have caused the world to be inundated
by injustice. Like a suitcase that has suffered a shampoo explo-
sion, all of God's good creation has been tainted by wicked disobedience. There is no escape from the present pain except
through salvation in and by the return of Jesus Christ—for
while Jesus' life, death, resurrection and ascension have initi-
ated salvation blessings for his people, it is only when Jesus

---

[4] Willem A. VanGemeren, 'Psalms', in *The Expositor's Bible Commentary*, ed.
Tremper Longman III and David E. Garland, Revised, vol. 5 (Grand Rapids:
Zondervan, 2008), 340.

returns and human history arrives at its culmination that full and final salvation blessings will be experienced. We will revisit the return of Jesus in more detail later, but it must be noted that only then will we be certain of escaping injustice indefinitely. In the present, multiple injustices are the Christian's constant companion.

At the time of writing there is a news story circulating social media about a pastor who was outspoken about some Pride events happening in his locality. His approach may have been a little lacking in wisdom, but in response LGBTQ advocates openly attacked him on social media. They went as far as to threaten to attack him physically and to burn down his church's building. Unsurprisingly the escalation led to police involvement. Rather than speaking to those who threatened violence, however, the police spoke to the pastor and asked him to soften his rhetoric. This is not the place to debate the nature of public opposition to socially acceptable practices that are unbiblical. Nonetheless, the police clearly should have been addressing those making public threats of violence—the pastor had simply expressed his biblical understanding that Pride events promoted a lifestyle that was not beneficial for society at large. We should see the experience of this ordinary pastor as a reminder that Christians are guaranteed to face injustice. It is to be expected. If the world hated Jesus, it will hate his followers (John 15:18-20).

It is not all bad news, however. Experiencing injustice should actually be a comfort to the Christian—especially if such injustice is a constant companion. It should be a comfort on two fronts. Initially, given Scripture's testimony that injustice is the Christian's constant companion, experiencing it should contribute to confirming our status as a Christian. We must be careful in this designation given that the entirety of creation is exposed to the consequences of the first sin. There are many unbelievers who suffer as much as or more profoundly than Christians. Nevertheless, it is true that Scripture affirms that Christians will suffer. Indeed, that Christians must suffer. The Apostle Paul, for example, explains that the Holy Spirit bears witness to our status as children of God, and thus fellow heirs with Jesus Christ, provided we suffer (Rom. 8:16–17). Or consider Peter's exhortation: "Do not repay evil for evil or reviling for reviling, but on the contrary, bless, for to this you were called" (1 Peter 4:9). Later Peter explicitly links this reviling to his readers' godly behaviour as Christians (4:16). Therefore, if in your righteousness you face the active hostility of the wicked, take heart. Believers cannot long be faithful in their discipleship without creating friction with the world with which they come into close contact. The Christian's constant companion, injustice, is one indicator that his salvation is genuine.

On the second front, it must also be acknowledged that injustice further refines the Christian's character. This too should be a comfort. James expresses this most memorably: "Count it all joy, my brothers, when you meet trials of various kinds, for you know that the testing of your faith produces steadfastness. And let steadfastness have its full effect, that you may be perfect and complete, lacking in nothing" (James 1:2–4).

Surely trials of various kinds include experiencing injustice, and in James' mind this provides the opportunity to grow in steadfastness. In other words, it refines our character. While James and Paul are often presented as incompatible or at odds with each other theologically, Paul makes precisely the same point in Romans: "we rejoice in our sufferings, knowing that suffering produces endurance, and endurance produces character, and character produces hope" (5:3-4). Once again sufferings undoubtedly include experiencing injustice. In Paul's thinking this experience, biblically understood, produces a refinement in character by building endurance and hope. The Christian's constant companion, injustice, is a key tool in the Creator's hand for purifying character. Matthew Henry captures how difficulties refine Christians: "Meekness suffers the word of admonition, and takes it patiently and thankfully ... Reproofs are likely to do us good when we meekly submit to them."[5] The constant companion of injustice has a purifying effect, like water washing sediment off a nugget of gold.

That God can use injustice to confirm our status as Christians and refine our character to Christ-likeness does not mean we welcome it with open arms. There should, indeed must be, a revulsion towards injustice. It is not the way God created or intended the world to be. The serpent in the Garden has much to answer for. The psalm which clearly influenced Jesus' third Beatitude, however, is frank about this reality—injustice abounds in our world.

Shining Most Brightly

Only in acknowledging the horrid nature of injustice do we begin to appreciate the relationship that exists between injustice and meekness. Injustice proves to be the canvas against which meekness shines most brightly. Bearing injustice is an expression of meekness. In fact, as Jerry Bridges points out, "One of the greatest tests of our meekness is the way we deal

---

[5] Henry, *A Discourse on Meekness and Quietness of Spirit*, 122, 124.

with the hurts dealt to us by other people."[6] We might add, especially when these hurts are the fruit of injustice—intentional actions to cause us harm. Meekness sparkles most brightly against the darkness of injustice.

As a student I was privileged to visit some missionaries working discreetly in Muslim North Africa. The small team was able to be there because they operated a travel business, using it strategically to visit particular restaurants or shops to build relationships. Part of my visit involved travelling into the mountains nearby. The excursion consisted of riding donkeys, swimming in mountain lakes and sleeping al fresco on flat rooftops. Wrapped up in a sleeping bag and some scratchy blankets, beyond the town limits and outside the reach of streetlights, I witnessed one of the most startling skies ever. Against the dark canvas of the black sky shone a million stars. The sky actually failed to be black, appearing a milky grey instead. The gentle twinkling of the stars was interspersed with the excitement of a shooting star. In my lifetime I have only seen a handful of comets shooting across the sky, almost all of them on that evening. It was mesmerising.

The same is true of meekness when witnessed against the canvas of injustice. It is mesmerising. Those who endure brutal injustice with the certain knowledge of their standing before God as Christians are remarkable. In a world in which every minor offence develops into another *hashtag* movement, those who suffer injustice with meekness shine most brightly. The reason for this is because the meek are found trusting God. John Piper aptly summarises: "Meekness is willing to take suffering. And it is so content in God, so confident in God, that it

---

[6] Bridges, *The Blessing of Humility*, 32.

rejoices in the suffering."[7] It is this trust in God, and this contrast between the bright shining stars and the bleak black background, to which we turn our attention in the next chapter.

---

[7] John Piper, 'How Do We Raise Kids Who Are Not Naive and Cynical?', Desiring God, accessed 14 December 2020, https://www.desiringgod.org/interviews/how-do-we-raise-kids-who-are-not-naive-or-cynical.

5
Two Destinies

Division

The world is irreconcilably divided. At least this is how it feels to me. I write as the close of 2020 approaches and reflect on a year in which the Black Lives Matter protests have divided not only the United States, but people across the world. I continue to watch as politicians, scientists and economists remain bitterly divided on the best approach to overcome Covid-19 and its ensuing chaos. Like many others I have been captivated by one of the most divisive US Presidential campaigns and elections ever—a statement that one would have thought unthinkable after the Clinton–Trump election dogfight. Writing in the United Kingdom also raises the spectre of Brexit and the fallout from attempting to extract oneself from a union. Everywhere we turn there is division.

In *Disciplines of a Godly Man* R. Kent Hughes shares the story of an Australian minister who took both Aboriginal boys and white boys on a bus trip. When they first got on the bus the white boys sat on one side and the Aboriginal boys sat on the opposite. Throughout the bus journey they traded insults with increasing ferocity. Eventually the minister had heard enough. He stopped the bus and made the boys get out. He then delivered the stern ultimatum that all the boys must identify themselves as *green* before getting back on the bus. One by one they agreed to identify as green and got back on the bus. As the minister recommended the journey he heard from the back of the bus: "All right, light green on this side, dark green on the other!"[1]

Hughes' story reminded me of one I heard from the British comedian (of Iranian descent), Omid Djalili. He studied English and Theatre at the Ulster University in Coleraine, Northern Ireland (not too far from where I live) in the 1980s. One of the extra-curricular activities that Djalili engaged in was football—and it was there, in true Northern Irish style, that he was asked whether he was a Protestant or Catholic Muslim! Ignorance and racism in equal measure (he is not even Muslim, but of the Bahá'í Faith). Yet the story highlights the innate desire in humanity to divide—are you one of us or one of them? The world appears irreconcilably divided and committed to continuing to divide.

It may then surprise us to find that Jesus also seeks to divide. Matthew records that Jesus said, "Do not think that I have come to bring peace to the earth. I have not come to bring peace, but a sword. For I have come to set a man against his father, and a daughter against her mother" (10:34–35). Jesus himself has come to divide. It is not so much that Jesus seeks to burrow his way into families and tear them apart, quite the opposite. The division Jesus speaks of here is a division caused by the message of the gospel. The division Jesus speaks of here is between those who believe the message of the gospel and those who do not. Jesus is teaching his disciples that they will encounter a sharp divide when they proclaim the good news of great joy in Jesus Christ. Truly the world is irreconcilably divided.

---

[1] R. Kent Hughes, *Disciplines of a Godly Man* (Wheaton: Crossway, 2019), 268.

Two Destinies

Division in the Biblical Worldview

In the biblical worldview there is a sharp division drawn. Such a division is categorised in a variety of ways, but it is always made on the same basis—faith.

An early division apparent in the biblical worldview is the division between God's people and the nations. After the primeval history of the cosmos, and with the call of Abraham, Genesis recounts how God created a people for himself and separated them from the nations (chapters 12–50). In the book of Exodus, despite living among another nation, God's people are distinct—living in their own quarters, enslaved and treated with derision by Pharaoh. Following the immense rescue from Egypt that God enacts for his people there is a mountain of laws given to them. These laws are recorded in the second half of Exodus, Leviticus, Numbers, and reiterated in the book of Deuteronomy. One of the primary purposes of these laws was to set apart God's people from the nations—to divide God's people from the nations. Moses declares:

> Keep them and do them, for that will be your wisdom and your understanding in the sight of the peoples, who, when they hear all these statutes, will say, "Surely this great nation is a wise and understanding people." For what great nation is there that has a god so near to it as the LORD our God is to us, whenever we call upon him? And what great nation is there, that has statutes and rules so righteous as all this law that I set before you today? (Deut. 4:68)

The division between God's people and the nations continues throughout the rest of the Old Testament. It is apparent in the narratives: judges empowered by the Spirit of the LORD

61

consistently deliver God's people from the surrounding nations. Subsequently, kings (with mixed success) fend off the nations from infiltrating God's people. It is apparent in the prophets: Nahum and Obadiah proclaim judgement on the nations, while Isaiah and Zechariah promise ultimate salvation for God's people. God's people are divided from the nations.

It should be noted that this division is not universal and absolute. Some from the nations join God's people. The obvious examples are Rahab the Canaanite (Josh. 6:25), Ruth the Moabite (Ruth 1:1) and Uriah the Hittite (2 Sam. 11-12). There are, however, also wider biblical principles for welcoming the foreigner, including laws for doing so (Lev. 19:33-34) and psalms which praise or anticipate such a reality (67; 87; 117). Even so, Scripture proceeds to continue to divide.

Later Old Testament literature then adds another layer to the division present in the biblical worldview, and this further revelation helps explain why some from other nations were welcomed into God's people. The wisdom literature in particular talks about the wise person and the foolish person. In the book of Proverbs, the wise are those who are devoted to God's word, carefully obeying it and knowing the blessing of such obedience (Prov. 2:1-15). Whereas, the fool is the complete opposite (1:7b; 10:1b). There is a progression beyond mere ethnicity with respect to division in the Old Testament. The division is between those who align themselves with God's word (the wise) and those who do not (the foolish).

The divisions of the Old Testament are then picked up in the New Testament but with further refinement as to the categories. In the Gospels this is exemplified in the difference between those who believe Jesus and those who do not. The division is between belief and unbelief. Matthew records the belief of the centurion who asserted that Jesus need "only say the word, and my servant will be healed" (Matt. 8:8) and sets that against the Pharisees and Sadducees who, in their unbelief, demanded a sign (16:1). Mark records the belief of the Syrophoenician women whose faith resulted in her daughter's healing (Mark 7:24–30) and sets this against the rich young ruler who apparently walks away from Jesus in unbelief (10:22). The pattern is repeated in Luke as Jesus shares the parable of the tax collector who in belief called out to God for mercy while the Pharisee in unbelief thanked God he was not like the tax collector (Luke 18:9–14). The Gospels employ the categories of belief and unbelief in continuing the biblical worldview of division.

In the rest of the New Testament literature, while all the above categories are present, it appears that the division is between the faithful and the unfaithful. The faithful are most often represented by individuals who have joined the Apostles in their ministry. Paul calls Timothy a "faithful child in the Lord" (1 Cor. 4:17). He proceeds to designate both Epaphras (Col. 1:7) and Tychicus (Eph. 6:21; Col. 4:7) as faithful ministers of the gospel. Onesimus is a faithful brother (Col. 4:9) according to Paul. Peter also refers to Silvanus as a faithful brother (1 Peter 5:12). Paul charges Timothy, his faithful child in the Lord, to entrust the gospel message to men who are similarly faithful (2 Tim. 2:2). The New Testament then closes with the Apostle John's revelation in which the church in Smyrna is charged to remain faithful unto death (Rev. 2:10) and there is the promise that the faithful will appear with Jesus Christ when final victory is realised (17:14). Throughout the New Testament those who are faithful are consistently referred to in a positive manner. On the other hand, those who live life to their own standard rather than God's are termed faithless. Paul does so at the end of Romans 1; after listing the vanity and vices engaged in by rebellious humanity, he labels them "faithless" (v. 31). Such a point of view is reaffirmed in Revelation 21:8 as the faithless are promised a second death in the lake of fire and sulphur that burns eternally.

Division is part and parcel of the biblical worldview. Just as a crowd of sports fans flocking to a stadium is easily divided by the colour of their team's kit, so the Bible easily divides humanity. On one side stand God's people: faithful wise believers. On the other side stand those who are not God's people: faithless foolish unbelievers. It is vital to note, however, that this division has nothing to do with any inherent merit in the individual—it is all to do with that individual's relationship to Jesus Christ. This is exactly the point made by Paul in Romans 5:12–21 and 1 Corinthians 15:21–24. In both passages Paul asserts that sin and death entered the world through Adam's disobedience, a disobedience all humanity participates in. This is mirrored in both passages by Paul's announcement that righteousness and life entered the world through Jesus' obedience, an obedience those trusting in Christ share. The division of the biblical worldview is founded solely on our relationship with Jesus. As the Puritan Thomas Goodwin famously noted, "In God's sight, there are two men—Adam and Jesus Christ—and these two men have all other men hanging at their girdle strings."[2] Reader, are you clinging to Adam or to Jesus?

---

[2] Quoted in F. F. Bruce, *Romans*, Tyndale New Testament Commentaries (London: Tyndale Press, 1963), 127.

The Righteous and the Wicked in the Book of Psalms

The importance of the individual whose coattails we have firmly clasped in our hands is made plain in the Psalter. Within the Book of Psalms, the constant division is that between the righteous and the wicked. It is set out in the very first psalm: the wicked keep company with sinners and scoffers (v. 1) which leads to their downfall of being blown away like chaff in the judgement of God (vv. 4–5); on the other hand, the righteous shun the wicked in favour of God's word (v. 1–2) and as a result flourish like a mature tree planted near a constant source of water (v. 3). While the wicked perish, the Lord knows the way of the righteous (v. 6). The division between the wicked and the righteous in the Psalter is a matter of life and death.

Such is the division in Psalm 37, the psalm which informed Jesus' thinking expressed in the third Beatitude. In Psalm 37 the wicked are designated evildoers, wrongdoers, ruthless, enemies, and transgressors. Their actions are always only against God, and yet have a devastating impact on God's people. Full of viciousness, the wicked in the Psalter physically attack God's people, lashing out at them with fatal intent. This is depicted in Psalm 37 with the image of them drawing their swords and bending their bows, all with the aim of taking down God's people (v. 14). In John Steinbeck's grim tale *East of Eden,* the narrator remarks: "I believe there are monsters born in the world to human parents."[3] He proceeds to define these monsters as those with "malformed souls."[4] Such are the wicked of Psalm 37 in particular, and the Psalter more broadly. Like ivy they creep imperceptibly across the path of the righteous, soon to strangle them (v. 35).

---

[3] John Steinbeck, *East of Eden* (London: Penguin, 2000), 74.
[4] Steinbeck, *East of Eden*, 74.

The wicked of Psalm 37 are set in sharp contrast to the righteous. In the psalm the righteous are the beleaguered—they are in the wicked's crosshairs as aim is taken. Perhaps surprisingly, the righteous are not exhorted to raise a sword in response to the wicked. Instead, the righteous of Psalm 37 are designated the meek (v. 11). Unlike the wicked who are active throughout the psalm, the righteous trust the LORD (v. 3), delight in him (v. 4), and wait patiently for him (v. 7). This is the shape of meekness—deferring one's rights in the present with the knowledge of what lies ahead. The righteous who are meek are assured abundant peace, an eternal heritage, divine protection and final deliverance and exaltation.

In the Psalter the wicked are fools who say there is no God (14:1). They have a firm grip of Adam's coattails and are unwilling to let go. The righteous, however, have thrown themselves on God (37:5) and know that there is no other option. Matthew Henry demonstrates the significance of this for meekness. He writes: "When the events of Providence are grievous and afflictive, displeasing to sense and crossing our secular interests, meekness not only quiets us under them, but reconciles us to them."[5] Such are the righteous in Psalm 37: quiet under the attack of the wicked because in meekness they are trusting God. As Henry proceeds to explain, "Meekness teaches us prudently to govern our own anger … it is the work of meekness to moderate our natural passions against those things that are displeasing to sense, and to guide and govern our resentments."[6] However, this is not possible without recognising the division in the biblical worldview.

[5] Henry, *A Discourse on Meekness and Quietness of Spirit*, 8.
[6] Henry, *A Discourse on Meekness and Quietness of Spirit*, 12.

Two Destinies

The Two Certain Destinies

The significance of division in the biblical worldview is directly related to the destinies of these two groups of people. Psalm 37 sets these out starkly for the reader.

The wicked are promised a certain destiny of doom. The psalm opens with the promise that those who do evil will fade away and wither like parched vegetation (v. 2). They will perish and vanish (v. 20). They will ultimately be destroyed (v. 38) and therefore cease to enjoy the ill-gotten life of comfort that they presently relish (vv. 10, 36). The imagery of the psalm is actually quite brutal and striking—suggesting that the downfall of the wicked comes about because their arms have been broken (v. 17). Throughout the psalm these arms have carried out evil actions (v. 7) and taken aim at the righteous (v. 14). Stealing (v. 21) is the purview of the wicked one, but those arms that once grabbed what they could are soon snapped and steal no more. All of this is summed up in the partial refrain echoed at four junctures in the psalm: the wicked will be "cut off" (vv. 9, 22, 34, 38). The destiny of the wicked is certain doom.

The righteous are confident of a different destiny. While they might only have a little (v. 16) there is no shame in it (v. 19), as there is more than enough to suffice and share (vv. 25–26). Rather, the righteous will enjoy peace (v. 11), because God will uphold them (vv. 17, 24, 31, 33) and establish their steps (v. 23). God will in no way forsake the righteous (vv. 25, 28). The full demonstration of such allegiance, and the ultimate destiny of the righteous one, is an enduring forever (vv. 18, 25, 27–29) in the land that God will grant (vv. 9, 11, 22, 34). As opposed to doom, the righteous are granted, indeed guaranteed, life. According to Psalm 37 the righteous are promised a very different destiny from that afforded to the wicked. In this they must be confident.

The Key to Meekness

Exactly how this all relates to meekness needs to be stated explicitly. Jesus' proclamation in the third Beatitude—that the meek are blessed for they will inherit the earth—can only be made on the basis that anyone who is not meek will not inherit the earth. Such an understanding emerges directly from Psalm 37 on the basis that there is a sharp division made throughout the entirety of Scripture between faithful wise believers and faithless foolish unbelievers. Psalm 37 makes it abundantly clear that the faithless foolish unbeliever, or the wicked to use the Psalter's predominant terminology, is destined to be cut off. The certainty of this destiny informs Jesus' proclamation. Likewise, the certainty that the faithful wise believer, or the righteous to use the Psalter's language, is destined for an inheritance that will endure forever informs the third Beatitude.

As witnessed earlier, these are not mere words for Jesus but a way of life. What else could restrain the all-powerful God of the universe from obliterating the fools who warmed their palms on his face? Consider God-in-the-flesh enduring a scourging that tore away the skin to expose the muscle. Picture him kneeling exhausted from pain as the soldiers fill their mouths with saliva before emptying them in his face. Imagine the dull thud as the crown of thorns is driven repeatedly into his head. How does Jesus resist from commanding the angelic host to strike down these blind minions of Satan? He has read Psalm 37. He knows their end. Jesus knows the destiny of the wicked. And as the only truly righteous one, he knows his own destiny. Death will not be the end. Comprehending the sharp division in the biblical worldview is imperative to both under-standing and imbibing meekness.

Eventually we have reached the point at which it is safe to pause and consider the injustices we have faced and the two destinies which may help inform our reactions to such circumstances. This word is especially for those within the church. It has been my experience that the Christian community, and especially leadership in that community, suffers a significant lacuna: meekness. This is scandalous given that Jesus himself both commanded and exhibited meekness. I find it truly remarkable that a defining grace such as meekness is roundly ignored. The sad reality is that far too frequently those in "Christian" leadership are often domineering, sometimes aggressive and are commonly found seeking to be served rather than serve. In many instances it seems these combative character traits are necessary to rise to the top. This is not only scandalous, but problematic.

The problem is that many damaged individuals are often left in the wake of such so-called leaders. I know. My theological formation took place under the tutelage of several celebrity Christian leaders who have now disqualified themselves from ministry by demonstrating, among other things, a severe lack of meekness in their leadership positions. I have therefore experienced, at a distance, the pain of this betrayal. There are others who have been on the coalface. There are some who have felt the spittle and hot breath of the raised voice and open mouth of a so-called Christian leader. Others have been shamefully ridiculed in public, and often with no opportunity for reply. And some have been assaulted physically or sexually by those who should have been protecting them.

Who are these wounded Christians to turn to? Who can salve the wounds and serve the weak? Who can draw alongside the victims in a way no other can? The obvious answer, according to Scripture, is Jesus Christ. Reread the passion narratives in the Gospels and know that Jesus has experienced all that you have. Consider the way in which Peter ties a quiet and godly life to the example of Jesus (1 Peter 3:8–22; 4:12–19). Endure injustice like Jesus.

If you have been burdened and battered by wicked so-called Christian leadership, I can assure you on the solid word of Scripture that your Saviour is not like these fallen "shepherds." I plead: do not abandon any connection to church in an attempt to protect yourself from the charlatans who claim to be Christian leaders. Run to the Saviour who is the full embodiment of meekness. More, know that there are under-shepherds who follow in the footsteps of the Great Shepherd, albeit imperfectly. If you have suffered at the hands of slavedrivers in shepherds' clothing I want to remind you of a greater shepherd who would die for you.

For those reading this currently in Christian leadership, beware the trap. The drift away from meekness is insidious. Our pride refuses to let us demean ourselves below our so-called station. Others must do the work that is below me. Such thinking is cancerous and sure to choke meekness out of existence. Commenting on Jesus' exhortation to his disciples to follow his example of lowliness (John 13:14), D. A. Carson warns: "One of the ways human pride manifests itself in a stratified society is in refusing to take the lower role."[7] Fellow shepherds, this is not the way of Jesus. Rather, "Jesus is emphatic that leadership

---

[7] D. A. Carson, *The Gospel According to John*, Pillar New Testament Commentary (Leicester: Apollos, 2010), 467.

in His kingdom is not about ordering people around, but about washing their feet. If we want servant-heartedness in the church, we can't shout about it from the pulpit."[8]

As much as leadership positions may attract us with financial and reputational appeal, "Christianity is not the gentle, easy-going thing that is sometimes mistaken for it; it is not a mere sentimental means of comfort in the troubles of life. It involves heroic self-denial."[9] If we are truly to follow Jesus' leadership, heroic self-denial is the standard under which we walk. Jonathan Edwards asserts that Jesus "is man as well as God, and he is the holiest, meekest, most humble, and every way the most excellent man that ever was."[10] We cannot match Jesus, but we should seek to emulate him with all his energy at work so powerfully within us (Col. 1:29). The certainty of two destinies must help us in this. Jesus could wash the feet of Judas, who would soon betray him, because he was certain of the ultimate destiny of them both (John 13:3). We too can endure injustice and exemplify meekness because of the certainty of a faithful wise believer's ultimate destiny. Perhaps before praying for revival demonstrated by conversions we might be better praying for revival demonstrated by an end of the all-too-common ugly assertiveness present in so-called Christian leadership. May God, by the power of his Spirit, make those of us in Christian leadership happily lowly, mightily meek and ultimately most excellent in every way.

The Christian community is awash with Christians who have been hurt and damaged by intimidating and domineering "Christian" leaders. Individuals who have sought to advance

---

[8] Jeremy McQuoid, 'An Antidote to Evangelical Leadership Cults', *Evangelicals Now*, December 2020, 32.

[9] Machen, *The New Testament*, 362.

[10] Quoted in Ortlund, *Gentle and Lowly*, 97.

themselves at the expense of others are not Christian leaders. If you have suffered at the hands of such people you need to know that this is not who Jesus is, nor who he asks his disciples to be. If you have behaved this way in Christian leadership repent now, knowing that Jesus is faithful and just to forgive you (1 John 1:9). For anyone who has been detrimentally affected by these poor examples of "Christian" leadership look to Christ's meekness and learn to seek out Christian leaders who are meek like Jesus. As difficult and as time intensive as it will be, learn to trust such leaders despite earlier experiences; it is necessary.

The character of Jesus' true followers is beautifully self-controlled: meek. There is no ugly assertiveness about them. I hope and pray that this will bring comfort and grace to you who have been scarred. The reality of injustice and the two destinies set forth in Psalm 37 are vital foundations on which to begin building this trust with others again. However, there is one more ingredient from Psalm 37 which is equally vital: God's justice. The meekness demonstrated by Jesus and the meekness demanded by Jesus from his followers shines brightly against injustice and secures an eternal destiny of hope and joy only because of who God is. Who God is, specifically in his holiness, is the focus of our next chapter.

6
One Judge

Half True, yet Still False

One of my guilty pleasures is *The Simpsons*. The main Simpsons cast is supported by hundreds of secondary characters who migrate in and out of storylines in different seasons. The lenient Judge Roy Snyder is one of those characters who reappears at frequent intervals. He is prone to letting culprits off the hook, often reasoning that boys will be boys. Two of the main characters, Homer and his son Bart, avail of Judge Snyder's leniency far too often. In one episode, however, just as Judge Roy Snyder is about to deliver yet another acquittal for Bart and Homer, his alarm clock sounds. This noise marks the beginning of Judge Snyder's vacation. The court is not left without a judge, however. Roy Snyder is replaced by Judge Constance Harm—the name gives the game away. Judge Harm is not lenient. She is a sadistic, unforgiving disciplinarian. If you have committed the crime Judge Harm will ensure that you do the time. And so, Bart and Homer find themselves facing a harsh punishment for whichever misdemeanour they were guilty of that week.

Judges Roy Snyder and Constance Harm effectively illustrate the two primary views regarding the God of the Bible. For many, the God of the Bible is a genial grandfather figure who is more than happy to look the other way in order to avoid displeasing anyone. For others, the God of the Bible is a vindictive, dictatorial figure whose only mission is to catch you in the wrong and then punish you to the maximum extent of the law. The genial god is often equated with New Testament teaching, while the vindictive god is often equated with Old Testament teaching. These two views of God are only half true and in being so, they are utterly false. According to the Bible there are not two judges, but one (Jas. 4:12). The one judge of Scripture, God, is perfectly fair in his generous grace and judicial justice. There is no imbalance in God.

Adopting a Mindset, Imbibing Meekness

If we are truly to adopt the Messiah's mindset, and thus imbibe meekness, we must know this one judge of the Bible and do so accurately. It is only in seeing God for who he truly is that we will be able to arrive at a point of happily deferring to others and their preferences. We must make Jesus' way of thinking ours. If, as we will argue below, God is the only perfect judge who impeccably balances grace and justice, then his people can forfeit their rights and preferences because they know in the end God will judge rightly. It was in this knowledge that Jesus entrusted himself to his Father (Matt. 26:36–46).[1] Knowledge of the Holy One is imperative for adopting the Messiah's mindset and imbibing the meekness demanded of disciples. In this way, "What comes into our minds when we think about God is the most important thing about us."[2]

To be truly meek demands a correct understanding of who God is. The Old Testament passage out of which Jesus develops the third Beatitude, Psalm 37, helpfully orientates our thinking to several facets that are vital in comprehending who God is. Two aspects in particular emerge from the psalm:

---

[1] Henry, *A Discourse on Meekness and Quietness of Spirit*, 27, encourages his readers to 'tread in the steps of the Lord Jesus, who, when he was reviled, reviled not again; when he suffered, he threatened not, but was as a lamb dumb before the shearers, and so committed himself to Him that judges righteously.'

[2] A. W. Tozer, *The Knowledge of the Holy*, Reprint (London: Authentic, 2007), 1.

holiness and judgement. It is these two aspects, taken together, that instruct us as to who our one judge really is. By introducing our holy defender, Psalm 37 aids its reader towards achieving the high calling that Jesus lays on his followers in the third Beatitude.

Our Holy Defender

It should strike us that the psalmist is careful not to portray God's defending his own people as a blind tribal allegiance. Rather, by continually placing God in opposition to the wicked and evil ones, the psalmist conveys the reality that God's defence originates in and emanates from his holiness. In the middle of the psalm, it is explicitly declared that "the Lord loves justice" (v. 28). The God of the Bible is holy, righteous, just, perfect and good—he is utterly unique. Adopting the Messiah's mindset and subsequently imbibing meekness is impossible without a right knowledge of who God is. We must see him as our holy defender.

The holiness of our defender is presented in more detail by the defence that he provides. The one who is meek can rest assured that God will defend him. Despite the apparent proliferation of enemies, God will vanquish them all (v. 20). Although the way of the wicked might allure wandering eyes, God promises his presence and protection for those who remain meek (vv. 27–28). Even though the righteous face a full-frontal attack, God will shield them from all that the wicked can throw at them (vv. 32–33). No matter how bleak the outlook, God will usher his people into a future glory beyond all comprehension (vv. 37–38). The character of our defender is demonstrated by his complete eradication of the wicked. Only in meditating on this can we hope to remain meek. If our holy defender will act decisively then we can refrain from fighting for our own rights at the expense of others.

Those who are not Christians find themselves in a perilous situation, however. The contemporary world cannot abide this language, but Scripture is clear: those who are not followers of Jesus are the wicked, evil ones and enemies described in Psalm 37. Alienated from the holy defender described in this psalm, those who are not Christians face his just judgement. In fact, every human faces his just judgement. But Christians have experienced forgiveness from sin through faith in Jesus Christ. I write this to warn those of you who are not Christians of the coming judgement depicted in Psalm 37 and to plead with you to consider the salvation Jesus Christ offers. Deliverance from just judgement is found only at the cross of Christ, where love and mercy met. In 1 Thessalonians 1:10 the Apostle Paul asserts that it is only Jesus who rescues us from the coming wrath. Surely this is injustice? No! Because of Jesus' meekness in deferring to the plan of the Father, thus dying on the cross for our salvation, we can be forgiven and made disciples. The plea is to avail of this forgiveness while you can, for at some point it will be too late.

Somewhat like the transition from Judge Roy Snyder to Judge Constance Harm, at some point the opportunity to avail of the forgiveness won by Jesus Christ will have passed. The day of reckoning will have arrived. At that point our judgement will depend wholly on whether we are a disciple of Jesus, trusting in him, or a disciple of self, trusting in ourselves. Throw yourself at the mercy of the holy defender and know the peace of sin forgiven and a future secure.

One Judge

The Waiting Game

Of course, the reality of our holy defender does not always mean things are straightened out in the here and now. Catching the news headlines is enough to disabuse us of this fairy tale. Unfortunately, we are forced to play the waiting game. The exhortations given to the reader at the beginning of Psalm 37 make this clear. The reader must place his trust in God (v. 3). The reader must commit himself to God (v. 5). The reader must be still and wait on God (v. 7). Patience is necessary.

James picks up on this very concept in his short letter:

> Be patient, therefore, brothers, until the coming of the Lord. See how the farmer waits for the precious fruit of the earth, being patient about it, until it receives the early and the late rains. You also, be patient. Establish your hearts, for the coming of the Lord is at hand. Do not grumble against one another, brothers, so that you may not be judged; behold, the Judge is standing at the door. As an example of suffering and patience, brothers, take the prophets who spoke in the name of the Lord. Behold, we consider those blessed who remained steadfast. You have heard of the steadfastness of Job, and you have seen the purpose of the Lord, how the Lord is compassionate and merciful. (Jas. 5:7–11)

James' argument in these verses is built on the first six verses of chapter 5. The "therefore" at the beginning of verse 7 makes this clear. The exhortation is built on the preceding, prophetic condemnation of the wicked rich. Since there will be judgement for the evil landlords who have defrauded, cheated and unfairly treated their poor tenants, James exhorts the suffering Christian community to which he writes to remain patient.

Importantly, James is addressing Christians. In the first six verses of James 5 the term "brothers" is noticeably absent, but in the following six verses it occurs four times. James has turned to address his brothers and sisters in Christ and to assure them of their holy defender. Employing the term "patient" twice in verses 7–8 reiterates James' point that patience is necessary.

The term used by James, however, describes an expectant waiting; waiting with an attitude of perseverance. It is not a sit back, wait and see, twiddle your thumbs kind of waiting. It is a militant waiting—waiting with action.[3] Therefore, James does not simply tell his readers to be patient because judgement is certain. Rather, by asserting that Jesus is coming back to execute justice, James is telling his readers to live in a particular way because there will be final judgement. He is calling his readers to live in light of the end. The waiting game is one in which God's people are called to participate.

As James makes clear, this demands that we live differently in the present (vv. 8–9). Jesus' return is always taught in Scripture with the implication that our behaviour must change in the present. The biblical authors always talk about the end of time so that we may live in light of the end. Eschatology is always taught to impact ethics. The final judgement is always mentioned with a view to changing our behaviour in the present. The difficulty we face is that we have to be patient for that end. James therefore exhorts his readers to be steadfast (vv. 10–11).

The militant waiting James calls for includes an enduring—remaining steadfast. By using examples James captures our attention. Both Job and the prophets are held out as models to

[3] Craig L. Blomberg and Miriam J. Kamell, *James*, Zondervan Exegetical Commentary on the New Testament (Grand Rapids: Zondervan, 2008), 226.

78

emulate. He chooses them as examples because they have been blessed for their steadfastness (v. 11). The blessing they received is an objective, unalterable approval and reward. This is explicitly demonstrated at the end of Job as God restores everything to him, indeed gives him more because of his steadfastness. James is calling the churches to which he writes to note the example of these men. Look at how they endured—remaining steadfast—and then remember God's rich blessing lavished on them. He is declaring that the end of time not only includes judgement for the enemies of God, but vindication and blessing for the people of God. James promises us that there is blessing for those who endure. Only in knowing this can we remain meek.

In considering meekness, Derek Kidner explains that the Psalm 37 "context gives us the best possible definition of the meek: they are those who choose the way of patient faith instead of self-assertion."[4] James articulates it in a slightly different way, but the truth is unchanged. The psalmist's world is a world full of injustice and hardships that test meekness to its full extent—it is clear that the wicked and evil are apparently successful (Ps. 37:1-2, 7). Similarly in James' world, the rich get richer, and the poor get poorer (Jas. 5:1-6). But the meek trust God, commit themselves to God and wait patiently on God to act. It is a waiting game.

Psalm 37, like Jesus and James subsequently, encourages us to be meek by employing patient faith. This is no futile exercise according to the author of the psalm. We are not called to defend our own rights, personal preferences or burning desires. Quite the opposite, we are called to forgo them and await our holy defender to act in his own time. John Piper notes:

---

[4] Kidner, *Psalms 1-72*, 168.

"Biblical meekness is rooted in the deep confidence that God is for you and not against you."[5] In our deep confidence that God is for us we recognise that full and perfect justice will one day be done (and be seen to be done) and all promised rewards will be lavished on the rightful recipients. Matthew Henry helpfully draws our attention to this reality:

> we have a righteous God, to whom, if in a meek silence we suffer ourselves to be injured, we may commit our cause, and having his promise that he will "bring forth our righteousness as the light, and our judgement as the noon-day," we had better leave it in his hands than undertake to manage it ourselves ... If there be any vindication or avenging necessary, (which infinite Wisdom is the best judge of,) he can do it better than we can.[6]

We can happily defer to the preferences of others in the present when we know that we have a holy defender whose perfect judgement will be made clear in the future.

Perceptive Perspective

Psalm 37 offers us a way to see the world from God's perspective. It is an insightful perspective and in it we see that there are values that last and bring certain rewards. It also reveals that there are some values that are transitory and destroy, even if at the time they look tempting. The values that last and make for peace are trusting God, committing to God and waiting on God—imbibing meekness. For those who do not imbibe meekness a look through this psalm points to an end that awaits the enemies of God—judgement.

---

[5] Piper, 'Blessed Are the Meek'.
[6] Henry, *A Discourse on Meekness and Quietness of Spirit*, 26–27.

The meek, however, look through this psalm and are assured that God will act to bring favour. For those days in which injustice infuriates your heart turn to Psalm 37. A meditation on this psalm will soon soothe those who are on the verge of discarding meekness. Our holy defender, who perfectly balances grace and justice, will one day bless the meek immeasurably for their steadfastness.

Adopting the Messiah's Mindset: A Summary

In this second part of the book, we have been exploring the idea of adopting the Messiah's mindset. We have learned that Jesus' teaching is rooted in the Old Testament. The third Beatitude and Jesus' teaching on meekness emerges from the text of Psalm 37 in particular. Concentrating on this psalm has taught us that multiple injustices will be the Christian's constant companion on this side of eternity. This is both a challenge and a comfort, but it is also the dark canvas against which meekness shines most brightly. In exploring the Messiah's mindset we have also discovered that the world is irreconcilably divided between the righteous and the wicked. Indeed, it is in this way that that meekness shines most brightly. Moreover, both the righteous and the wicked have certain destinies. The wicked are assured doom, while the righteous are assured life eternal. Finally, we considered the presentation of God as our holy defender in Psalm 37 and James 5. It is God alone who sees all and judges all (Heb. 4:13), and who will do so perfectly. The Messiah's mindset is the right view of God and a right view of the world.

The blessings which the meek will enjoy if they endure are the focus of part three. There we will see that the meek will eventually share in messianic majesty by sharing Jesus' inheritance and rule. Only our holy defender can manifest that reality, but when he does we will know that refusal to assert oneself over others will have been worth it—we will experience with exuberant joy the blessedness promised to the meek.

Part Three:
Sharing Messianic Majesty

7
Eternal Inheritance

Just Passing Through?

At the risk of bursting your bubble, heaven is not your ultimate hope. Chubby, winged babies strumming harps will not be the soundtrack to eternity. The sky is not the Christian's final destination. We are not just passing through this world. Yet, sadly, far too frequently Christians consider heaven their eternal destiny. We believe that we are just passing through this world— waiting to be promoted to better things. Such a concept is encapsulated in an old Negro spiritual song:

> This world is not my home, I'm just a-passin' through;
> My treasures are laid up, somewhere beyond the blue.
> The angels beckon me from heaven's open door,
> And I can't feel at home in this world anymore.[1]

I whole-heartedly agree with the sentiment, and likewise long to be free from this present evil age (Gal. 1:4). The sad reality, however, is that such loose phraseology has misguided many. Christians are not headed ultimately for heaven but for a new creation. Our eternal inheritance is tangible. It will resemble this world, just as our resurrection bodies will resemble our earthly bodies. Anthony Hoekema explains

---

[1] As quoted in Christopher J. H. Wright, *The God I Don't Understand: Reflections on Tough Questions of Faith* (Grand Rapids: Zondervan, 2008), 194. In his book Wright has the opening line as 'This heaven' but the well-known hymn reads 'This world'. Nevertheless, he proceeds to make the same argument I am making here.

Matter is not evil; it is part of God's good creation. Therefore, the goal of God's redemption is the resurrection of the physical body, and the creation of a new earth on which his redeemed people can live and serve God forever with glorified bodies. Thus the universe will not be destroyed but renewed[2.]

The Bible asserts that Christians are guaranteed an eternal inheritance. The inheritance Scripture speaks of is the new earth. Everlasting life on a resurrected, glorified earth is our ultimate hope, final destination and eternal home. We are not just passing through.

The Promise in the Beatitude
It is easy to read the third Beatitude and focus entirely on the call to be meek. Indeed, that is what we have done thus far in this book. But it would be short-sighted of us to miss the promise attached to this call, "Blessed are the meek, for they shall inherit the earth" (Matt. 5:5).

Meekness is a blessing in itself. As Matthew Henry highlights, "Meekness is gainful and profitable."[3] Even so, Jesus, in all his goodness and grace, goes as far as to attach a promise to this Beatitude. Despite being a blessing in itself, it is attended by a further blessing in the form of a promise: the meek will inherit the earth. Such a promise is significant.

The significance of this promise is that it guarantees the meek all that the assertive and overbearing trample others to gain: everything. As the character Samuel Hamilton astutely observes in Steinbeck's *East of Eden*, "There's a capacity for

[2] Anthony A. Hoekema, *The Bible and the Future* (Carlisle: Paternoster Press, 1994), 250.
[3] Henry, *A Discourse on Meekness and Quietness of Spirit*, 61.

appetite that a whole heaven and earth of cake can't satisfy."[4] He is not talking about belly-rumbling hunger, but rather the insatiable desire for that little bit more—whether fame, riches or sex. Is this not why people abandon meekness and live a life of taking what they can get at the expense of others? There is an appetite that cannot be satisfied even though it possesses all it can want. Adam and Eve demonstrate this impeccably in the Garden of Eden by crunching into the one thing they could not have in the whole earth. The bold and brash have an insatiable appetite. But the promise attached to the third Beatitude beckons its reader or hearer to forsake the pursuit of more and embrace meekness. Indeed, in light of our sinful hearts and attitudes, it necessitates meekness to find satisfaction in what we have been given. Those who by the grace of God embrace meekness are promised the whole earth by Jesus in the third Beatitude.

Vaughan Roberts argues, "God's ultimate goal is not just to save a people, but to put everything right so they have a perfect place to live in."[5] The third Beatitude makes the same argument. The true disciple is not simply meek but is promised life in a world that is populated by other meek disciples—a perfect place to live in—a new earth. Such is the eternal inheritance and messianic majesty in which the meek are ensured a share.

Living in the Land

The promise Jesus attaches to the third Beatitude is not original to him. As we have already noted, this Beatitude is a quotation of Psalm 37:11. For those who are meek, the promise

---

[4] Steinbeck, *East of Eden*, 159.
[5] Vaughan Roberts, *Life's Big Questions: Six Major Themes Traced Through the Bible* (Leicester: Inter-Varsity Press, 2004), 121.

threaded throughout Psalm 37 is that their inheritance is living in the land with the LORD.

It is asserted in Psalm 37 that the meek will dwell in the land (vv. 3, 29) for they will inherit the land (vv. 9, 11, 22, 29, 34). It is the Promised Land that is being referenced here in the psalm. The land in which God promised to place his people; the land flowing with milk and honey; the land of abundance and peace, joy and fulfilment: such is the land that is being promised to the meek. It is a land that lacks nothing. To put it another way, it is a land that contains all that is not only necessary, but that can be desired. The psalmist encourages his readers with the promise that those who forsake their own rights and trust in God will inherit the Promised Land in all its fullness.

Contrast this promise of blessing with the promise of judgement for those who are not meek. Psalm 37 repeatedly warns that the wicked will be cut off from the land (vv. 9, 22, 28, 34, 38). In virtually every verse in which this cutting off is mentioned it is set in direct contrast to inheriting the land. The implication is that the wicked will be shut out from this land. God's judgement is to exclude them from all that they have been pursuing ceaselessly at the expense of others.

Even a cursory reading of the Old Testament reveals that the Promised Land is a central concern. A land is promised to Abraham when God calls him from Ur (Gen. 12:1). The entire book of Deuteronomy is located on the edge of the Promised Land. There Moses reiterates the importance attached to entering and remaining in the land—nothing less than God's glory is at stake (5:24-27). Both Joshua and Judges describe the fierce battles waged in order to take and keep the land. Moreover, judgement on Israel is made tangible by exile (Deut. 30:1-10)—being cut off from the land.

The aim and the hope of the Old Testament believer was to live in the land in which God lived. The Promised Land was the destination towards which all Old Testament believers marched. It is the dream destination that they would have punched into Google Maps had it been available. Psalm 37 promises that such a land is the inheritance of the meek.

Old Testament Hope Reappropriated

The promise of Psalm 37, and the Old Testament more broadly, is reappropriated by Jesus and the New Testament authors. It is not that they discard the promise of a land, but they build upon and develop it. Paul Williamson explains: "the Bible does not hold out the prospect of some extraterrestrial life with God in 'heaven', but rather of heaven on earth, where God will live eternally with us."[6] The New Testament clarifies this prospect. It is not the Promised Land we long for, but heaven on earth.

Consider the third Beatitude. Notice, it is not the land but the earth that is promised to the meek. With Jesus' teaching "The pious Israelites who inherit the land have become the meek followers of Jesus who inherit the whole earth."[7] After all, this is one element of the model prayer that Jesus teaches his disciples: "Your kingdom come, your will be done, on earth as it is in heaven" (Matt. 6:10). Is this not a prayer for the new creation to arrive in all its beautiful fullness?

The writer to the Hebrews picks up on the hope of inheriting the earth in his discussion of Abraham and his most immediate descendants in 11:13–16. In these verses the author to the

---

[6] Paul R. Williamson, *Death and the Afterlife: Biblical Perspectives on Ultimate Questions*, New Studies in Biblical Theology 44 (London: Apollos, 2017), 27.

[7] Craig L. Blomberg, 'Matthew', in *Commentary on the New Testament Use of the Old Testament*, ed. G. K. Beale, and D. A. Carson (Nottingham: Apollos, 2007), 20.

Hebrews reminds us that all of these descendants died without inheriting the Promised Land. However, he proceeds to clarify that in fact they were holding out for a better land—a heavenly land, as Hebrews puts it. Once more, this is not some ethereal existence that is desired. Life lived in God's presence was their ultimate hope. In his second letter, the Apostle Peter explicitly teaches his readers that we are looking forward to a new heaven and a new earth in which righteousness dwells (2 Peter 3:13). Life will be lived perfectly in God's presence for all eternity only in the new heavens and the new earth. Finally, John reveals the arrival of this new heaven and new earth in Revelation 21.

There is of course so much more that could be said about how the New Testament authors build on the promise of the land in the Old Testament. Nevertheless, the above is sufficient to demonstrate that they do. Old Testament hope is re-appropriated. Our future hope must now be delineated.

The New Heavens and the New Earth

It is right that Christians do not feel at home in the here and now. As Paul makes clear at the beginning of Galatians, this present age is evil (1:4). But our escape from this present evil age is not heaven. We must be careful that our language does not suggest this. It is the mistake Iain Murray makes when writing, "earth, however blessed, will never begin to equal heaven … This world will never be the Church's rest."[8] In many ways Murray is correct, but to be truly accurate we must assert that while earth in its present state can never begin to equal heaven,

---

[8] Iain H. Murray, *The Puritan Hope: Revival and the Interpretation of Prophecy*, Reprint (Edinburgh: Banner of Truth, 2009), 218.

this earth in its future state will be where the church of God rests. It will be on earth as it is in heaven.

Murray's mistake could be likened to seeing your family and friends at a wedding ceremony. No one turns up to a wedding in their day-to-day clothes. The gents squeeze into slimming suits, while the ladies wrap themselves in dazzling dresses. At first glance people look unfamiliar. But pause a moment and we soon begin to recognise familiar faces that have been "remade" in their wedding attire. It is not that our family and friends have disappeared, it is simply that they have been, in a manner of speaking, re-created. Of course, the transformation that earth will undergo will be much deeper and truer than the external decoration we engage in for a wedding. The new earth cannot go back to its old look, as we will the day after the wedding. It will be new. Equally, however, there will remain some recognition that it is in fact the earth that has been remade. It will be dazzlingly different—new—but we will know it as earth.

Such a future is only possible because of the birth, life, death, resurrection, ascension and return of Jesus Christ. His work makes it possible. All things have been reconciled by Jesus Christ (Col. 1:20). J. Gresham Machen explains that "The end of the reconciliation will be a new heaven and a new earth."[9] As Paul provocatively portrays it in Romans 8, the whole of creation is groaning and creaking under the weight of this evil age (ourselves included). The answer to this is not discarding this world, but its being re-made through the renewal that Jesus makes possible for all of creation in addition to humanity. The new heavens and the new earth are our eternal inheritance.

---

[9] Machen, *The New Testament*, 164.

Isaiah's prophecy speaks explicitly of this new heavens and new earth to come (65:17–25). In this passage, which is arguably the high point of the prophecy, Isaiah declares that God will be at his creative work once more (vv. 17–18). This new creation will be a place where there is no weeping (v. 19). Life will be enjoyed to its fullest (v. 20) and the abundance of delights enjoyed (vv. 21–22). There will be no enmity (v. 25). The entirety of this new creation will be populated with the meek— God's happy subjects. Isaiah is making the very same argument we have been making in this chapter: the Christian hope is inextricably linked to the earth, for it is promised to the meek. Elsewhere, I summarise Isaiah's conclusion in this way:

> For the Christian, this means that our ultimate hope is not tied up in this world. Our ultimate hope is not tied up in the things we experience with our five senses. Rather, our hope is tied up in something yet to come in all of its fullness. Our hope is tied up in new heavens and a new earth that are flawless. Our hope is tied up in new heavens and a new earth that are redemptive because only God's people will be there. Our hope is tied up in new heavens and a new earth that are righteous because all sin and evil will be vanquished.[10]

Isaiah's prophecy is picked up again by the Apostle John in the book of Revelation. The vision recorded by John demonstrates how some of the features we have noted in this chapter are fulfilled in God's new creation. The new heavens and the new earth will be where God dwells with his people (Rev. 21:3). Since they find themselves in his perfect presence there will be

---

[10] S. D. Ellison, *The Holy One of Israel: Exploring Isaiah* (Independently Published, 2019), 53.

Eternal Inheritance

no more sadness, sickness, suffering or sin (v. 4). All things have been made new (v. 5). This heritage, it is promised, belongs to those who have conquered (v. 6). Desmond Alexander writes, "As the book of Revelation reveals, there is yet to come a time when all that is evil will finally be removed from the present earth. At that stage, when God makes all things new, his presence and glory will fill a rejuvenated earth"[11].

But as the rest of Scripture demonstrates, this conquering is not done by the strong, instead it is accomplished by those who refuse to assert themselves and are therefore considered weak in the world's eyes (1 Cor. 1:18–31). By this stage, however, I hope we know better—the ones who will inherit the new heavens and the new earth are actually the strongest of all, for they are meek.

Our Eternal Inheritance

For those who hear Christ's call to be meek, and follow it no matter the cost, there is huge encouragement. The promise is that the meek will inherit the whole earth. Everything that we have forsaken in deferring to the preferences of others; every denial of self for the good of another; every sacrificial act of self-control will be rewarded with all that could be needed and desired. Our consolations will more than make up for our tribulations.

Desmond Alexander argues that "The hope expressed in the Beatitudes resembles the eschatological hope of the Old Testament prophets (cf. Isa. 61:1–3)."[12] This statement proves true for both the community characterised by the Beatitudes

---

[11] T. Desmond Alexander, *From Eden to the New Jerusalem: An Introduction to Biblical Theology* (Grand Rapids: Kregel Academic, 2008), 18–19.

[12] T. Desmond Alexander, *The City of God and the Goal of Creation*, Short Studies in Biblical Theology (Wheaton: Crossway, 2018), 149.

and the promises attached to them. Surely such a promise should give us the encouragement needed to persist in our endurance in meekness. As Rudolf Stier claims: "Self-renunciation is the way to world-dominion."[13] Is this not what Jesus promises? Blessed are the meek, for they will inherit the earth.

The meek are thus promised a share in Jesus Christ's messianic majesty. They are in line to inherit all that he will inherit as the rightful king enthroned at God's right hand. Rather than escaping this world, they will win it back in a resurrected, glorified state that the Bible designates as the new heavens and the new earth. If we are among the meek Jesus promises us the world.

Inheriting this promise is only possible because we are joint heirs with Christ and this is his inheritance. Our final chapter explores this concept.

---

[13] Quoted in, John R. W. Stott, *The Message of the Sermon on the Mount*, Second Edition, Reprint, Bible Speaks Today (Nottingham: Inter-Varsity Press, 2008), 44.

8

Royal Heirs

Kingly Instincts

In my living room stands a most comfortable wingback chair. It sounds fancier than it is, having been sourced from IKEA. Nevertheless, I love it. This chair is my reading chair, it is where I sit to watch football on TV and it is the chair that most visitors choose to sit in—if I do not get there first.

Two visitors in particular enjoy the chair: my twin nephews. At present they both fit on it as they snack on treats while watching cartoons. After the sugar rush from their snacks (and at my instigation, it must be confessed) they are not so keen to share the chair. Instead, all three of us grab one another's limbs, drag each other from the chair, clamber up ourselves and proudly proclaim: "I am king of the chair!" The cycle of new kings of the chair repeats itself ad nauseum until I regret starting it. Mercifully, it generally ends in fits of laughter rather than fits of tears—generally.

The simple game reveals the kingly desires that lie within each one of us. Humanity possesses an innate desire to rule and reign. Given God's command to the first humans this is hardly surprising. After creating Adam and Eve God charges them to "have dominion" (Gen. 1:26, 28). The word translated dominion appears elsewhere throughout the Old Testament communicating the idea of ruling—often in the context of kingship or kingdoms. In addition to commissioning humanity to have dominion, God also creates them in his image (Gen. 1:27). Desmond Alexander argues that this too points to a kingly rule. He suggests that in the ancient Near East kings were commonly viewed as a living image of a god. He therefore concludes that "To be made in the 'image of God' is to be given regal status."[1] All of us have been created, in some sense, to rule.

In a fallen world this desire to rule and reign is perhaps the primary reason that humanity so willingly rejects meekness — albeit from a mistaken understanding of what actually constitutes meekness. The common misconception is that meekness is a synonym for weakness. It is therefore, in the minds of many, an obstacle to be overcome in the drive to rule and reign. It is a weakness to suffocate in the cultivation of power. Steamrolling others by brute force is what is necessary in order to rule and reign, or at least that is the general understanding. Again, this should not surprise us, especially given all that happened in the Garden of Eden. Adam and Eve's disobedience resulted in a distorted dominion. This distorted dominion has been rampant ever since, bringing destruction and spiritual death to many.

Our kingly instincts are not wrong. It is their application that has been warped by sin. The messianic majesty promised to those who are meek provides the intended outlet for these kingly instincts. Rather than riding roughshod over others, our desire to rule and reign should be done in conjunction with Jesus' rule and reign. Thus done, it will bring blessing to both ourselves and others. Therefore, this final chapter intends to fill out our eternal inheritance by recognising that we are royal heirs on the coming new earth.

The Kingship of Jesus

The Gospel according to Matthew, in which we find the third Beatitude, is particularly keen to demonstrate that Jesus is

---

[1] Alexander, *From Eden*, 77.

king. It begins with Jesus' birth. As Matthew constructs his nativity narrative, he starts with the declaration that Jesus is "the son of David" (1:1) and follows that with a genealogy to prove it (1:1–16). The prophecy that Mathew argues has been fulfilled in Jesus' birth is a prophecy about a coming king (Matt. 1:23; cf. Isa. 7:14). These arguments are soon followed by the assertion that Jesus' birth in Bethlehem is the fulfilment of yet another prophecy related to Davidic kingship (Matt. 2:6; cf. Mic. 5:2). All of these details in the nativity narrative alert the reader to the kingliness of Jesus. Furthermore, "Son of David" is one of the most distinctive titles for Jesus in Matthew's Gospel. It is used nine times, eight of which are unique to Matthew (1:20; 9:27; 12:23; 15:22; 20:30, 31; 21:9, 15; cf. Matt. 22:42 and Mark 12:35). For Matthew's readers, if Jesus is to be recognised as the Messiah, he must be the one God has raised up from David's line to take David's throne and establish an eternal Davidic rule. It is this proposition that Matthew sets out to prove.

Other New Testament authors are also keen to make this apparent. From the outset of Romans, for example, Paul makes it clear that Jesus is descended from David (Rom. 1:3). Paul then proceeds to employ the title Christ repeatedly throughout the letter. The term Christ undoubtedly carried kingly connotations. Thus, the use of a kingly title and the assertion of Davidic ancestry clearly marks Jesus as king. Additionally, Paul also identifies Jesus as the son of God (Rom. 1:4). This filial relationship between Jesus and the Father echoes Old Testament passages in which God promises to father the promised king (2 Sam. 7:14; Ps. 2:7; 89:26–27).[2]

---

[2] This paragraph is indebted to The Gospel Coalition essays "Jesus as Messiah" and "The Messianic Hope" by T. Desmond Alexander.

Jesus is undoubtedly king. Moreover, he is the long-expected king. As we have been learning in this book, however, his kingship is of a very different order from that of other kings—especially in the ancient Near Eastern culture in which Jesus operated. The Old Testament books of Samuel document the emergence of kingship in Israel. While showing readers both the best and the worst of human kingship, the books of Samuel highlight some aspects that will identify the true king God has promised. Desmond Alexander explains that "the narrative envisages the ideal king as one exalted from humble origins who demonstrates absolute trust in and obedience to God."[3] Such a description fits none other than Jesus. Humanly speaking, Jesus came from humble origins (John 1:46) and demonstrates absolute trust in and obedience to God (Matt. 26:36–46).

United to the King

Kevin DeYoung asserts: "Union with Christ may be the most important doctrine you've never heard of."[4] This assertion is no overstatement. He continues:

> The whole of our salvation can be summed up with reference to this reality. Union with Christ is not a single specific blessing we receive in our salvation. Rather it is the best phrase to describe *all* the blessings of salvation, whether in eternity past (election), in history (redemption), in the present (effectual calling, justification, and sanctification), or in the future (glorification).[5]

---

[3] T. Desmond Alexander, *The Servant King: The Bible's Portrait of the Messiah* (Vancouver: Regent College Publishing, 2003), 70.

[4] Kevin DeYoung, *The Hole in Our Holiness: Filling the Gap between Gospel Passion and the Pursuit of Godliness* (Wheaton: Crossway, 2012), 94.

[5] DeYoung, *Hole in Our Holiness*, 94.

Union with Christ is the technical theological terminology for our relationship with Jesus as Christians. It is not so much that he enters our hearts as that we live in him (although Christ does live in us, see John 14:20).

The concept of union with Christ conveys the reality that through conversion Christians are joined to Christ. All the blessings of salvation belong to Jesus and so flow to us through our being united to him. Just as marriage joins two individuals together, so salvation joins us to our Saviour. Whenever the New Testament talks about this reality it often uses the preposition "in" followed by Christ, Jesus or him. Thus, we can say that Christians are crucified (Gal. 2:20), buried (Col. 2:12), baptised in death (Rom. 6:3), raised (Rom. 6:5) and found (Phil. 3:8-9) in Christ. Believers are one with Jesus (John 17:26). To summarise, we are blessed in Christ with every spiritual blessing (Eph. 1:3).

If Jesus is king, as the New Testament certainly claims, we are not only united to our Saviour but united to our king. In Ephesians 2:6 Paul notes that God has "seated us with [Christ] in the heavenly places in Christ Jesus." The significance of this line lies in understanding that being seated with Christ in the heavenly realm is a position of great honour, prestige and power. It is the seat of kings. By being united to the king we are granted to take our seat with him. Although this is yet to happen, it is so certain that Paul can speak of it as if it has already happened. Such certainty arises from our union with Christ. Only through this union are we granted this privilege. However, because Jesus is already seated in the heavenly realms, our joining him is certain. We are united to the king.

Joint Heirs

No matter how godly we are I would guess with confidence that we have all dreamed about becoming heirs to some great estate. After all, imagine what you could do with all that money—clear your debt, fund a missionary, enjoy a family holiday, build a church, own the dream car, give away Bibles. The reality is we are more likely to find ourselves in the funniest cartoon that Warren Wiersbe ever saw. It depicted a pompous lawyer reading the last will and testament of one of his clients. Surrounding the lawyer is a group of greedy relatives. The caption to the cartoon read: "I, John Jones, being of sound mind and body, spent it all!"[6]

The New Testament, however, is explicit about the fact that Christians are joint heirs with Jesus Christ. He has spent none of the inheritance—it remains intact for his people. In Romans 8 Paul encourages the Christians in Rome with the gloriously good news that the Holy Spirit bears witness that they are children (v. 16). If they are children, Paul reasons, they are heirs (v. 17). Moreover, they are joint heirs with Jesus himself (v. 17). The same truth is reiterated in Galatians—in Jesus Christ we are heirs (Gal. 4:1-7). Just as King Jesus is the Son of God, so too Christians enjoy sonship to the degree that we can confidently cry "Abba! Father!" (Gal. 4:6).

The writer to the Hebrews likewise picks up on this theme and explains that while humanity does not have dominion over creation at present, one day we will (Heb. 2:6-8). It will be so because through Jesus Christ's suffering and death (v. 9) many sons will be brought to glory (v. 10). Once more sonship, kingship and inheritance collide in promise. Desmond Alexander writes:

---

[6] The story is told in Wiersbe, *Be Rich*, 29.

Throughout these verses, the author of Hebrews is speaking of humanity ('man') in general. He anticipates a time when their status as viceroys will be re-established and everything will be subject to them ... By becoming a perfect human viceregent in the present, Jesus Christ is able to re-establish the viceregent status of other human beings in the future.[7]

The same is communicated elsewhere with the image of the elect participating in Jesus' exercise of judgement on the last day. Paul's rhetorical question in 1 Corinthians 6:2 suggests this: "Or do you not know that the saints will judge the world?" Jesus also appears to make this promise to at least the 12 disciples, if not to all those who follow, in Luke 22:29–30: "I assign to you, as my Father assigned to me, a kingdom, that you may eat and drink at my table in my kingdom and sit on thrones judging the twelve tribes of Israel."

Being joint heirs with Christ will lead to many blessings, all of them better than any estate a rich uncle or yet unknown ancestor can leave us. The most pertinent of them in relation to the content of this book is the fact that we are joint heirs to ruling in the kingdom of God.

Royal Heirs

Implicit since its inception is humanity's status as royal heirs. Having been created to rule and reign, the hope of our eternal inheritance is to rule and reign aright. Despite Adam and Eve's disobedience which introduced a distorted dominion that corrupted human kingship into using power to control others, all was not lost. In and through King Jesus, humanity's kingly instinct was corrected and our position as royal heirs both

---

[7] Alexander, *From Eden*, 93–94.

asserted and secured. But, like all heirs, we must wait truly to enjoy what is rightly ours. For, "although the kingdom of God (the reign of Christ) is a present reality, the consummated kingdom awaits his return in glory. Only then will the viceregency of all believers be fully and perfectly established."[8]

Sharing Messianic Meekness: A Summary

In these final two chapters our share in the messianic majesty has been outlined. The meek, those who have learned messianic meekness and adopted the Messiah's mindset, are assured a share in messianic majesty. In the first place, this majesty consists of an eternal inheritance that encompasses the new heavens and the new earth. All that has been forsaken in the pursuit of meekness will be inherited in perfection. The true majesty is that the meek will not simply exist there, but rule as kings with the True King, Jesus.

---

[8] Alexander, 95.

Conclusion:
Paradoxical Promises

A Taste for Power

There is an apparently innocuous advertisement for chicken that carries a deceptively destructive message. The advert is for Fridge Raiders chicken. A woman named Julie eats some Fridge Raiders chicken, which, we are told, is packed with protein. As a result, she develops a taste for power. This is visualised as she power-dresses with a professional trouser-suit, with power shoulders (really just 90s shoulder pads) and finished off with power-hair (simply the biggest perm you have ever seen). Julie then begins to play power-ballads on power-keys while power-walking on a power-boat. The advert ends with the tagline: get a taste for power. We may smirk, but this innocuous advert carries a deceptively destructive message that is effectively the mantra of our world.

Desmond Alexander captures the danger of the Fridge Raiders advert: "People captivated by wealth and power are divorced from God."[1] An appetite for power is not something a Christian should seek to satisfy. Quite the opposite. Christians should strive to cultivate a character marked by meekness. Instead of being a victim of an assault by a wet noodle, our world repeatedly mutters the mantra: get a taste for power. But Jesus does not see it this way and therefore neither should we, his disciples.

---

[1] Alexander, *From Eden*, 184.

Learning, Adopting, Sharing

As became clear when learning messianic meekness in Part One, an aversion to meekness is nothing new. The Jews of Jesus' day sought to satisfy an appetite for power. They dreamed of once more establishing themselves as powerbrokers. Yet, into this feverish moment of first-century heightened expectation Jesus interpolates: "Blessed are the meek, for they shall inherit the earth" (Matt. 5:5). In this statement Jesus explains that divine favour which leads to deep joy rests on those who possess an inner strength, based on their relationship with Christ, that enables them to act for the benefit of others, even at their own expense. As Christians we bear the name of this meek and lowly Jesus Christ and thus should follow his example. Jesus not only teaches on meekness but demonstrates it with open arms (Matt. 11:28–30) and royal humility (21:1–11). What Jesus taught he lived. There is a pertinent lesson for would-be leaders in the Christian community: Christian leaders are subject to King Jesus, the meek Messiah, and would do well to both truly know and genuinely emulate our king. We do not simply obey Jesus' orders; we follow his example. We are learning messianic meekness.

In Part Two we considered how we might adopt the Messiah's mindset. The first step plunged us into the Old Testament. The third Beatitude directly quotes from Psalm 37:11. Initially, Psalm 37 confronts the reader with the sobering reality that injustice is the Christian's constant companion, but against this bleak backdrop meekness shines most brightly. Psalm 37 continues the theme of contrast outlining the two very different destinies that await the righteous and the wicked. Such a division is part and parcel of the biblical worldview. The certainty of this division and the resultant destinies is what

Conclusion

gives shape to meekness. To be truly meek demands a correct understanding of God our holy defender, poised to execute a full and final perfect justice. By carefully attending to the third Beatitude's Old Testament context, we can begin to adopt the Messiah's mindset.

In Part Three we learned that the reward for meekness makes this light and momentary suffering pale in comparison to the weight of glory yet to be revealed (2 Cor. 4:17). This glory is not some ethereal hope, but a tangible hope. Christians are assured a home in the new heavens and new earth wherein righteousness dwells (2 Peter 3:13). Indeed, that the meek will inherit this glory is the explicit promise of the third Beatitude. Our conviction about our eternal inheritance rests not only in God's word, but also Christ's work. Surely such a certain promise should give us the necessary encouragement to persevere meekly. The ultimate reward entails not merely a place in the new creation, but a throne there. The meek are royal heirs of the coming new earth. United to Christ we are united with the undisputed king. And our future ruling brings to fruition God's original creation design. Implicit since creation's inception is humanity's status as royal heirs. Having been created to rule and reign, the hope of our eternal inheritance is to rule and reign aright in the messianic majesty we will share (Ps. 8; Heb. 2:5-10).

In Our Time

In surveying the rampant abuse of power prevalent in our time it is not difficult to see why the world takes issue with Jesus' third Beatitude. More surprising is the apparent issue that many Christians take with Jesus on this point. Abuse, bullying, one-upmanship and the frenetic jostling for power within

Christian circles is deflating to watch and devastating to experience. What are we to do?

Near the beginning of *The Lord of the Rings* trilogy Frodo suddenly feels the weight of the task lying before him. He complains to Gandalf, "I wish it need not have happened in my time."[2] Gandalf responds, echoing Frodo's feelings before counselling: "and so do all who live to see such times. But that is not for them to decide. All we have to decide is what to do with the time that is given us."[3] We may likewise wish we did not live through this particular period where domineering leaders seemingly abound and appear to face few if any repercussions for their antics. But such decisions are not ours to make. As another fictional character explains, "The Good Lord does not play dice, as a certain physicist once said. Nothing happens by mere chance in the cosmos."[4] The question is therefore how will you live in our time? For it is here and now that God has placed you.

In our time meekness is a glaringly absent characteristic in Christian communities. It should not be so. As Martyn Lloyd-Jones observes, "Where there is a complete absence of humility and lowliness, there is no Christianity at all."[5] This is not a call to roll over and give up. No. It is a call to meekness. It is a call to forgo one's own rights for the benefit of others in light of all we have learned, adopted and will one day share through our union with Jesus Christ. It is a call to be thoroughly Christian. In the introduction to Lloyd-Jones' book *Magnify the Lord*,

[2] J. R. R. Tolkien, *The Lord of the Rings* (London: Harper Collins, 2001), 50.
[3] Tolkien, *Lord of the Rings*, 50.
[4] Pierre Boulle, *Planet of the Apes*, trans. Xan Fielding (London: Vintage Books, 2011), 165.
[5] D. Martyn Lloyd-Jones, *"Magnify the Lord: Luke 1:46-55"* (Ross-shire: Christian Focus Publications, 2011), 102.

Conclusion

Russell Moore notes that Lloyd-Jones was once designated the "gentle steamroller."[6] This is what I am calling for in our time: Christians who are resolute enough not to be shipwrecked, but gracious enough to defer to others even at their own expense— to be known as gentle steamrollers. My prayer is that every one of us would be characterised by meekness.

Our job is not to trend on twitter and take down the establishment. According to Jesus, we are to shine brightly against a bleak backdrop, and in shining brightly to be part of a quiet revolution. This revolution does not take to the streets but kneels behind closed doors. It does not rage against the machine but seeks out the single stray sheep. The emergence of true meekness does not begin in someone else, but in me. We are the ones responsible for what we do in our time.

The Paradoxical Promise

If, however, we can bear this light and momentary affliction of imbibing meekness we will prepare for ourselves a weight of glory beyond all comparison. Indeed, we are looking not to the things we can see, but all that is as yet unseen. It is what is as yet unseen that is truly eternal (2 Cor. 4:17–18).

The discovery we have made in this book is that "The beatitudes in the Gospels continue to praise the same character traits and spiritual virtues that are praised in the Old Testament, but the promised rewards are overwhelmingly spiritual and eschatological (to be fulfilled in the age to come)."[7] Psalm 37 promises the one who remains meek by trusting in God alone that they will one day live in the land. Jesus promises the one who remains meek an eternal inheritance over which they

---

[6] Lloyd-Jones, *Magnify the Lord*, 6.
[7] Ryken, *Jesus the Hero*, 133.

will rule. As Karen Swallow Prior highlights: "the Sermon on the Mount doesn't merely praise these qualities, it offers a paradoxical promise in which all of those who are last shall be first."[8]

The paradoxical promise remains: "Blessed are the meek, for they shall inherit the earth" (Matt. 5:5).

---

[8] Karen Swallow Prior, *On Reading Well: Finding the Good Life through Great Books* (Grand Rapids: Brazos Press, 2018), 231.

Acknowledgements

This book is dedicated to three individuals who have been significant influences on me over the past six years or so. Tom was an elder in Antrim Baptist Church as I commenced ministry there as Associate Pastor. He took a keen interest in me, offered me much encouragement, challenged me gently and provided considerable wisdom whenever I faced significant decisions. In all our interactions I have been struck by your meekness, Tom—I am indebted to your example. Sarah and Desi were my supervisors for PhD studies, and I am now Sarah's colleague in the Irish Baptist College. Both are wonderful biblical scholars who taught me so much about scholarship, Scripture and character. Your patience and grace as I battled my own limitations in the hope of producing work worthy of your supervision was exemplary. In all our interactions I was witness to and the recipient of meekness. Sarah and Desi, thank you for your quiet, pervasive impact on me. I am grateful to the Lord that he has permitted me to know all three of you.

A single sermon, preached in Strandtown Baptist Church in 2019, was the catalyst for this book. Thank you to Strandtown for the invitation to preach on meekness, forcing me to confront an aspect of biblical teaching I had thus far avoided. As I worked on this book both Tom Moore and Ben Davis read either all or significant portions and offered helpful feedback. Matthew Kelso and Nathan Blair also commented on some of the material. I am always grateful to anyone willing to read anything I write—thank you gents for your willingness and help.

My wife Tracy reads virtually everything I write and listens to essentially everything I preach. She knows better than most the inevitable gap between what I say and what I do—especially when it comes to meekness—yet loves me still. Indeed, she helps me close that gap. God has been so merciful in giving me such a friend and partner in love, life and ministry. I love you.

This book is only seeing the light of day because H&E Publishing were willing to make it happen. I am grateful to Chance Faulkner for his help and patience as I pitched this project to him, to Kayla Wester whose careful editing brought greater clarity to my writing and for the team at H&E who have so expertly guided me through the publishing process. May God continue to bless your ministry.

Above all I am blessed to have a meek Saviour who invites me to rest in him. My prayer is that this book might glorify him, edify you and in doing so help us embrace our God-given meekness and majesty.

Scripture Index

Scripture Index

21:8   64

Milton Keynes UK
Ingram Content Group UK Ltd.
UKHW031113080824
446563UK00001B/75